Crisis as a Political and Economic Concept

Ekrem Yaşar Akçay / Habip Demirhan / Selim Demez
(eds.)

Crisis as a Political and Economic Concept

A Multidisciplinary Approach

PETER LANG

Bibliographic Information published by the Deutsche Nationalbibliothek
The Deutsche Nationalbibliothek lists this publication in the Deutsche Nationalbibliografie; detailed bibliographic data is available online at http://dnb.d-nb.de.

Library of Congress Cataloging-in-Publication Data
A CIP catalog record for this book has been applied for at the Library of Congress.

This study was supported by Hakkâri University, The Coordinatorship of Scientific Research Projects

ISBN 978-3-631-79833-1 (Print)
E-ISBN 978-3-631-80347-9 (E-PDF)
E-ISBN 978-3-631-80348-6 (EPUB)
E-ISBN 978-3-631-80349-3 (MOBI)
DOI 10.3726/b 16203

Peter Lang – Berlin · Bern · Bruxelles · New York · Oxford · Warszawa · Wien

This publication has been peer reviewed.

www.peterlang.com

Contents

Preface

A crisis can be defined as a situation in which physical, social, economic, and political incidents disrupt the normal order, and which may produce negative societal consequences. Crises often necessitate that significant decisions are made under the normal system and society, and these decisions typically take place in the context of significant time pressure and stress. Although a crisis describes a turning point in life, this milestone can represent a positive change and an opportunity for growth. However, dangers are associated with crises in terms of difficulties and destruction. In this sense, crises represent the end of a period and the beginning of a new era, and they bring with themselves both risks and opportunities.

Therefore, successful crisis management is possible when both risks and opportunities are managed. Importantly, an approach to crisis management that focuses only on risks, dangers, and negative issues contributes to an inadequate crisis solution. In turn, this produces alienation, hopelessness, disrupted relationships, and destructive consequences. Contrastingly, a crisis management approach that focuses on the opportunities arising from the crisis provides a positive crisis solution. In this study, crises and their political and economic effects were discussed, drawing on the statements of experts with different dimensions and perspectives.

To elucidate the concept of crisis from a multidisciplinary standpoint, various bodies of research were included in this study, each of which was produced by academicians from Hakkâri University's (HU) Faculty of Economics and Administrative Sciences. Each academician discussed the concept of crisis in the context of different case studies. It should also be noted that this study was supported through the coordination of scientific research projects at HU. With these considerations in mind, the authors and we would like to express our gratitude to HU's Rector, Prof. Dr. Ömer Pakiş, who contributed to and supported the study.

Editors

Hakkâri/Turkey, 2019

Acknowledgment

The contributing authors of this work and we would like to express our sincere thanks to ***Hakkâri University*** (Turkey) for its financial, motivation, and encouragement in support of this project.

Editors

List of Abbreviations

ADF:	Augmented Dickey Fuller
BCA:	Başbakanlık Cumhuriyet Arşivi
CBRT:	Central Bank of the Republic of Turkey
CDO:	Collateralized Debt Obligation
CDS:	Credit Default Swaps
CHP:	Cumhuriyet Halk Partisi
CIA:	Central Intelligence Agency
DP:	Demokrat Parti
ECOFIN:	Economic and Financial Affairs Council
EDDS:	Electronic Data Delivery System
EEC:	European Economic Community
EFSM:	European Financial Stability Mechanism
EPB:	Energy Performance of Buildings
ERM:	Exchange Rate Mechanism
ESM:	European Stability Mechanism
EU:	European Union
EURATOM:	European Atomic Energy Community
FBI:	Federal Bureau of Investigation
G-7:	Group of Seven
GDP:	Gross Domestic Product
GNP:	Gross National Product
IMF:	International Monetary Fund
IMKB:	Istanbul Stock Exchange
JDP:	Justice and Development Party
LPM:	Linear Probability Model
NATO:	North Atlantic Treaty Organizations
OPEC:	Organization of Petroleum Exporting Countries
PATRIOT:	Provide Appropriate Tools Required to Intercept and Obstruct
SDIF:	Savings Deposit Insurance Fund
SEC:	Security and Exchange Commission
TBMM:	The Grand National Assembly
TL:	Turkish Lıra
UK:	United Kingdom
UN:	United Nations
UNCC:	United Nations Compensation Commission
UNSC:	United Nations Security Council
US:	United States

USSR:	Union of Soviet Socialist Republics
VAT:	Value Added Tax
WB:	World Bank
WW1:	The First World War
WW2:	The Second World War

Introduction

This book deals with a series of topics with a primary focus on political and economic crises. The content of the book is designed with a multidisciplinary approach. The book begins with US intervention in Iraq as a political crisis and Gulf Crisis as political crisis while the following chapters explore the economic and social crises.

Chapter 1 – The chapter aims to explore the fact that the European Union did not have a common attitude during the US intervention in Iraq in 2003.

Chapter 2 – The neorealist approach is tested by means of the case study starting with the 1990 Gulf Crisis and resulting in the war of 1991 due to creating imbalance in the international system. In light of the basic arguments of neorealism, it is put forward by this case study what can happen in the event of a crisis unbalancing the international system. In general terms, it is observed by the case study that the international system dominates World politics. This study elaborates on neorealist arguments within the framework of the Gulf Crisis and its repercussions.

The Gulf Crisis emerged after the end of the Cold War and functioned as a litmus paper for the structure of the international system and the powers dominating the international system (primarily the USA). It is deemed suitable to explain this crisis where the international system comes to the fore through neorealist arguments. The purpose of this study is to test the neorealist approach on the basis of the 1990–1991 Gulf Crisis. The assumption of the study is that if a state has material power and opts for extending its borders and sphere of influence against the system, this expansion effort will be prevented by various mechanisms since it will threaten the balance in the system. Indeed, the invasion of Kuwait by Iraq paved the way for an international crisis, and the Gulf Crisis was quenched by a military intervention led by the powers dominating the system.

Chapter 3 – The urban population has been growing rapidly for many years. The fact that cities become the center of economic life nourishes this situation. The rapid migration from the countryside leaves the cities in a difficult situation. Especially the lack of infrastructure and irregular construction make urban life difficult. A great economic resource is needed to solve these and similar problems. Economic competence is not only required to meet basic needs. Today's urban people have different demands and needs. Social facilities, green areas, cultural activities, clean, and wide streets are the elements of strong demand. All these elements are important in terms of determining the quality of urban life. Meeting the ever-changing demands of urban people requires an economic competence. It can be seen that periodic crises make it difficult to meet these demands. However, the impact of economic crises on urban quality of life is not limited to this. Increasing unemployment rates and falling incomes affect the individuals negatively. This situation negatively affects people as well as causing deterioration of living standards.

Chapter 4 – The agreements that established European Coal and Steel Community, European Economic Community, and European Atomic Energy Community have been the basis for the establishment of European Union. Nowadays, the European Union (EU) is claimed as the largest political and economic integration. In 2010, Eurozone faced with debt crisis. The future of EU has been questioned after this crisis within the context of Maastricht criteria. The study aims to explain the measures taken by both member states and the union to overcome the results of the crisis.

Chapter 5 – The necessity of having a small share of the public expenditures in the economy has long been defended. Especially with the development of capital after the industrial revolution, liberalism has strengthened. As a result of the great crisis, the confidence in the liberal economy has decreased. In this period, the public sector came to the fore. The end of the economic recession together with public expenditures increased the confidence in the public sector. But it soon became clear that this was a mistake. With the neoliberal policies, the understanding of free market has gained importance again. Today, it is accepted by a large group that the public sector is kept within certain limits. The inefficiency of the public sector seems to be accepted.

In spite of all these, it is seen that the public sector maintains its size. There are undoubtedly many reasons for this situation. However, as one of these reasons, ironically, the private sector can be seen. Increasing risk appetite of the capital, rapid borrowing, and uncontrolled growth disrupt the financial structures. Therefore, the effects of the crises are very big. In order to get rid of the chaos, public intervention is expected. Public sector is needed because the private sector cannot establish an auto control system.

Chapter 6 – In recent years, globalization, financial liberalization, and technological developments have experienced many crises throughout the world. These crises, which are usually caused by monetary reasons, are very costly to the economies of the country. In this chapter, the theoretical and empirical monetary crisis literature that emerged in the light of the financial crises in the past were examined. Thus, it is aimed that the types and reasons of monetary crises and the reasons for the monetary authorities and the ones who will work on the subject are aimed.

Chapter 7 – In "Turkey's First Devaluation: 7 September 1946 Decisions", Turkey's first devaluation of 7th September Decisions are examined, with a focus on the state's expectations from the decision and the practical consequences of the devaluation. 7th September Decisions is one of the most important economic events in the Turkish economic history in 1946. Turkey's foreign trade opportunities in the postwar period had narrowed. After the Second World War, the new order began to be established, pioneered by the United States, and in order to participate in this order, Turkey needed to make a number of changes. 7th September Decisions are the measures taken by Turkey to join free market after the Second World War and to adapt to the new economic policy that were implemented in the world. The aim is to increase the exports by removing the price and quantity constraints on foreign trade, and through limited increase in imports, lowering the price of export products in dollars.

Chapter 8 – Studies about whether current deficit can be accepted as a signal of a crisis have increased as from the 1990s. There is not a consensus on this issue as well as some of the authors think that national economies in which high current deficit is seen become more open to the crises. According to several authors, current accounts have not a great effect on crises. With reference to literature, the ratio of current account deficit to GDP needs to be 4 %–6 % and the related value is the threshold. This study aimed to test the causality relationship between the current account deficit and currency crises by using quarterly data of 1998Q1–2017Q2 period. The causality relationship between series is tested by Granger (1969) Causality Test and bootstrap causality test proposed by Hacker and Hatemi-J (2012). According to causality test results, there is a causality relationship from currency crises to the current account deficit in Turkey. These results prove that the current deficit cannot be evaluated as a leading indicator to estimate the currency crises for Turkey.

Chapter 9 – The study has considered marketing communication activities during crisis process in the chapter. Therefore, not only the costs, but also the investments have been examined in this book. Managers often perceive marketing investments as unnecessary during crisis process. However, it must be known that effects of crisis can be solved by marketing communication activities. In several examples, organizations used communication in order to promote their crisis management principles. Crisis is not just about economy; it is also about corporate reputation. So, thanks to the author for to contributing this book in a different area.

Chapter 10 – It is obvious that globalization eliminated the boundaries between countries and also made their economies dependable on each other. Financial markets have affected this process both positively and negatively. Although developed countries have strong and stable economies, developing countries have more fragile and weak economies. Therefore, financial instability can create domino effects in emerging markets because growing of these economies depends on trade with major economies.

This study aims to discuss the causes of global crisis in 2008 and effects on the Turkish banking sector and financial markets. However, this study mainly focuses on the effects of the 2008 financial crisis on Turkish banking sector. Sometimes, it refers to 2001 Turkish financial crisis because it is important to understand how Turkish banking sector stay strong during this period. In addition, in order to compare with its peers, financial structure and some financial ratios are analyzed and given examples from other emerging markets.

Assoc. Prof. Dr. Ekrem Yaşar AKÇAY

I The Effectiveness of the European Union in the Iraq Crisis in 2003

Abstract: This study aims to examine the fact that the European Union did not have a common attitude during the US intervention in Iraq in 2003. The European Union, which is called a bee that cannot make honey, could not produce a common policy in the 2003 Iraq intervention. Countries such as Britain and Denmark supported the US intervention in Iraq, and countries like Germany and France opposed the intervention. This situation caused a significant crisis within the EU. In this study, firstly, the changes in US foreign policy and the process leading to the Iraqi intervention will be mentioned. Then, the Iraqi operation will be discussed and it will be stated that the EU is not a monophonic structure. Finally, the reasons for this crisis experienced by the EU will be discussed and suggestions will be made.

Keywords: European Union, 9/11 Attacks, US, Iraq, Political Crisis

Introduction

The date of 9/11, 2001, is an excellent example of how the course of international relations, a state's foreign policy priorities, and security policies can change very quickly, with their effects spread over an extensive period of time. The attacks of 9/11 have an unprecedented quality. They are a non-state affair, and even though the US was chosen as a target, it was actually an attack against the point where Western civilization came from (Cox 2002, p. 249).

After the attacks, the foreign policy and security policies of the United States began to change. The United States, which emphasizes the need to tackle global terrorism, has supported and condemned terrorism (Thrall and Goepner 2017, p. 13). The U.S., which changed its security strategy to combat terrorism, labeled the states that support terrorism as enemies and announced that it would engage these states and organizations before terrorist organizations started their activities. Therefore, American troops were sent to Afghanistan to fight al-Qaeda, which was held responsible for the 9/11 attacks, in the country which had supported it (CIA 2003).

After the intervention in Afghanistan, US decided to intervene in Iraq by claiming that Iraq produced chemical weapons and supported terrorism. It was stated that Iraq was in the hands of a dictator—i.e., Saddam—that democracy would be brought to Iraq through the intervention, that the governments in countries that support terrorism would be terminated, and that welfare and peace would be instated in the region. It was in this context that the Iraqi intervention started on March 20, 2003, and the Saddam regime was overthrown (Pan 2005).

These events, which took place after the 9/11 attacks, seriously affected the EU and its member states. The multi-dimensionality of the threat of terrorism has forced the EU to reorganize and plan its defense. In this sense, foreign security, defense, justice, and internal policies were directly affected by the fight against terrorism (Council on Foreign Affairs 2011).

Along with the enlargement of the EU, all problems directly or indirectly related to terrorism have been included in the Union's issues. After the 9/11 attacks, terrorist activities in the EU countries obliged the EU to produce new policies within the Union and cooperate with international organizations in the fight against terrorism (Smyrl 2007, p. 120).

The EU, which condemned the 9/11 attacks and announced that it will provide all kinds of support in the fight against terrorism, experienced an important crisis during the Iraq intervention. Owing to its decision-making and institutional structures, the EU, which is described as a dragon playing with its head separately, has not developed a common policy against the Iraqi operation (Lindstrom 2003, p. 237). States such as Britain, Poland, Hungary, and the Czech Republic supported the intervention, while Germany and France opposed the operation. In other words, the EU did not have a common policy or act in a single voice against this operation owing to differences of opinion within itself (Oltermann 2018).

This study tries to explain the crisis caused by the political failure of the EU after the invasion of Iraq. A joint decision cannot be taken on issues concerning the vital interests of states owing to the EU's decision-making mechanism and institutional structure. This causes a crisis within the EU, an economic giant, which makes the EU a political and military dwarf. On the other hand, due to the structure in question, the EU is unable to adopt a monophonic structure, making it a bee that cannot make honey. In this context, this study will examine how the EU experienced this crisis during the Iraq intervention and the EU's reactions to it. It is not possible to evaluate the September 11 attacks, the US intervention in Iraq, and the policies of the EU in a quick and succinct manner. However, due to editorial restrictions, the ineffectiveness of the EU intervention in Iraq has been discussed in a general framework.

September 9/11 Terrorist Attacks and Change in US Foreign Policy

The terrorist attacks in the United States on September 11, 2001, have been a turning point in the political history of both the world and the US. On the

September 11, a Boeing 767 passenger airliner, which took the Boston–Los Angeles flight, was abducted with 81 passengers and 11 crew members. The hijackers hit one of the Twin Towers of the World Trade Center in Manhattan, New York. Shortly after that, a Boeing 757 passenger plane, en route from Washington to Los Angeles, hit the Pentagon, the head of the US Department of Defense, and the building collapsed. The third airplane that was kidnapped crashed in Pennsylvania. In all, 2795 people lost their lives that day. As the loss of life and property after the attacks were almost equal to what would have been lost in an attack on the US with regular troops, security measures were increased all over the country and President Bush called on emergency forces and reserve military units (White Paper 2016, p. 66). The Pentagon, known as the heart of US defense, which has a strategic importance for the US, and the attacks on the Twin Towers, known as the heart of US capital, showed that the US' security concept and security structures needed to be reviewed (Biddle 2005, p. 2).

After this incident, the foreign policy of the US began to change. The US has begun to take new security measures against this danger, known as the asymmetric threat, and about the loss of small actors, such as terrorist groups in the international system (Coats 2018, p. 12). Today, terrorism is perceived by the US as the greatest threat for national security and countries that support terrorism are known as the axis of evil. It is these countries that have been emphasized in the fight against terrorism (Leffler 2003, p. 1050).

After the 9/11 attacks, UN General Assembly Resolution 56 denounced the attacks and called for international cooperation (United Nations General Assembly 2001). At the same time, the UN Security Council adopted Resolution 1368, which emphasized the need to use all available means to combat terrorism to maintain international peace and security. The UN Security Council has also stated that its citizens and states are entitled to individual and collective right of self-defense (Rosand 2004, p. 587). The UN, condemning the incidents, said these incidents threatened peace and security and that the UN Security Council was ready to fulfill obligations under the UN Treaty (United Nations Security Council 2001). On the same date, NATO also condemned the incidents and announced the enaction of Article 5 for the first time in its history.

On September 15, 2001, President Bush made a speech in which he stated that America was at war and that those involved in these events would be punished and brought to justice (*The Guardian* 2001). In the following days, Bush said in his speech at the Congress on September 20, 2001, that the US would pursue the countries that supported the terrorists (*The Washington Post* 2001).

After the attacks, Bush said there was evidence that bin Laden had carried out the incidents and wanted the Taliban administration to deliver all elements of al-Qaeda in Afghanistan to the US, to shut down terrorist camps in the country, and to protect American citizens and foreigners. If these demands were not met, the Bush administration said the Taliban administration would be perceived as being allied with al-Qaeda. The Taliban administration, on the other hand, condemned the events and said that there was not enough evidence that al-Qaeda had carried out the attacks (Gohel 2017, p. 60).

On September 28, 2001, the UN Security Council adopted Resolution 1373. In this decision, individual and collective right of self-defense were approved and binding obligations were placed on member countries to prevent the financing of terrorism, to prevent financial support to terrorist groups, to examine and freeze the assets of terrorist organizations, and to repeat the call for cooperation (United Nations Security Council 2001).

However, the events of September 11 showed the US's deficiencies in the field of intelligence. In addition to the fact that intelligence agencies did not have sufficient information and equipment, the lack of communication between the agencies caused the events to reach this level. For this reason, on October 2, 2001, the PATRIOT Act (Provide Appropriate Tools Required to Intercept and Obstruct Terrorism-Patriot) was enacted (Teather 2003). This law has four fields of application:

- Knowledge acquisition and sharing
- Criminal law and its implementation
- Hardening of criminal penalties
- Border control and immigration procedures (U.S. Congress 2001)

Although this law has been enacted in the context of the fight against terrorism, it also includes provisions for the use of various computer programs to increase the jurisdiction of money laundering, listening, and search permits. In this context, both the fight against terrorism and the weakening of civil rights and freedoms have been addressed. The main basis of the law was to limit the rights and freedoms of the civilian population in the fight against terrorism. The law gave the government the power to recognize any group as a terrorist (U.S. Congress 2001).

On October 3, 2001, NATO member states stressed that they would make every effort to combat terrorism and acknowledged the following:

- Ensure intelligence sharing and cooperation in combating terrorism.
- Help members of the Alliance develop their ability to combat the threat of terrorism.
- Take necessary measures to increase the security of the members' territory.

- Provide the necessary equipment in areas under NATO's security responsibility.
- Ensure safety in air transportation.
- Allow members to provide the necessary benefits in military bases in NATO territory (Bennett 2003).

On October 4, 2001, the UK government issued a document titled Responsibility Certificate for Terrorist Atrocities in the United States on September 11, 2001, which the US approved. In this document, Osama bin Laden's background and his relationship with the Taliban Government were included (The British Prime Minister 2001). The United States began to bomb Taliban targets in Afghanistan on October 7, 2001, with the support of Britain. During this operation, known as Operation Enduring Freedom, President Bush made a speech to the nation and called on governments the U.S. had declared unlawful (CNN 2001). In mid-December 2001, the U.S., UK, and NATO forces took control of Afghanistan. The capital was under Coalition control and the Taliban forces were defeated.

In 2002, the U.S. National Security Strategy, known as the Bush Doctrine, was published. This document was intended to destroy potential threats before they became active (The White House 2002). The Bush administration stated that the new security strategy was prepared to glorify human dignity and to ensure the security of the world against terrorism and weapons of mass destruction (Santos & Teixeria 2003, p. 137). Countries with the ability to provide nuclear weapons to terrorists are also included in the definition of the war on terrorism (The White House 2002). In fact, this new strategy of the U.S. began with the dissolution of the USSR after the Cold War. With the end of the Cold War, it has left it to multidimensional and low-intensity conflicts such as civil conflicts and international terrorism instead of the possibility of a high-tension military conflict that threatens peace. The U.S. felt a false sense of security after the end of the Cold War (The White House 2002). For this reason, the Bush administration changed its perspective on terrorism after the attacks of 9/11. Terrorism, which has a more ideological structure than in the 1970s and 1980s, became more about religion in the 1990s. It also became a more global phenomenon, rather than centralized to a specific region (Spencer 2006, p. 7).

To this end, it has set limits on human rights to establish a better security system. Because the surpluses in freedom and democracy in the US are thought to provide important opportunities for the preparation and implementation of the actions of terrorists. On the other hand, it has shaped its internal security structure according to its new security perception. (Jenkins 2001, p. 8). For example, a reform law passed through the Congress combined with the CIA, which deals with external security incidents, and the FBI, which is responsible for internal security, within the Ministry of National Security (Coats 2017, p. 20).

Iraq Intervention of US in 2003

Iraq, after the events of September 11, has not been on the US agenda. On January 2002, President Bush never mentioned Iraq until his address to the nation speech at the Congress. In a speech he made on September 17, 2001, Bush said there was no evidence that Saddam Hussein had been involved in the 9/11 attacks (*The Guardian* 2001). Similarly, Condoleezza Rice also said that there was no clear evidence that Saddam Hussein had anything to do with the attacks of 9/11 (Leading to War 2001). But Bush, under the influence of the new conservative structure, has started to give messages about Iraq since January 2002. On January 29, 2002, Bush, who gave a speech known as the Union of the Nation on the axis of evil, has included Iran, Iraq, and North Korea within the axis of evil (The White House 2002). On June 1, 2002, Bush spoke of preventive war in his speech (North and Vann 2002). In a speech to the UN General Assembly on September 12, 2002, Bush said that the UN intervention in Iraq was inevitable as long as the UN is not taking action on the issue, referring to the UN resolutions that Iraq has so far violated. In this sense, Bush emphasized that the UN should act together with the United States to take a decision that would destroy Iraq's weapons of mass destruction (United Nations 2002). In his speech in Ohio on October 7, 2002, Bush tried to gain public support for the intervention in Iraq and said that he was in cooperation with al-Qaeda. Bush, Iraq's weapons of mass destruction in the hands of voicing Turkey and Israel also damage other than the US, has argued that Saddam's let them do their blackmail (American Rhetoric 2002).

These speeches signaled that the US will intervene in Iraq. For the US, which ended the 1991 Gulf War without entering Baghdad, Iraq has been isolated and remains a threat despite being subjected to UN sanctions. In fact, the US has supported the Kurds, the Shias, and the Iraqi National Council against the Iraqi administration by imposing a strict embargo on Iraq since 1993 and aimed at overthrowing the Saddam administration. However, after the attacks of 9/11, the Bush administration, which included Iraq in the evil axis, had a coalition to be formed without the permission of the UN Security Council on the grounds that it was a terrorist on October 25, 2002, had violated the rules on disarmament, and used its chemical weapons irresponsibly officially announced to intervene (Hulse and Mitchell 2002).

The UN Security Council adopted Resolution 1441 of November 8, 2002, which foresees that Iraq would face serious consequences if a time violation of its obligations under Article 687, adopted on April 3, 1991, following the first Gulf War (United Nations Security Council 2002). On February 5, 2003, US Secretary of State Colin Powell claimed that the UN control plans did not work and that Iraq had hidden weapons of mass destruction.

Operation Iraqi Freedom, organized by the United States and Britain, began on March 20, 2003. Two hundred thousand US troops, 429 tanks, and 500 combat aircraft and 435,000 Iraqi troops, 2600 tanks, and 300 fighter jets participated in the operation. France, Germany, Russia, and China have long urged the UN Security Council to stop the attack. American and British forces faced resistance during the operation in Shiite areas in southern Iraq. These difficulties in Umr Kasr, Basra, Nasiriyah, and Najaf caused doubts about the duration of the operation. The operation was over when the US troops entered Baghdad on April 9–10, 2003 without any resistance and US president George W. Bush declared the official end of the war on May 1, 2003 (United States Army Reserve 2013).

The US announced the aims of the occupation by overthrowing the Saddam Hussein regime, reaching the weapons of mass destruction, liquidating terrorist groups in the region, controlling Iraqi oil and energy routes, and making Iraq a model for Middle Eastern countries. The first direction of the US troops entering from Kuwait was the capital Baghdad. Along with the night bombers, the soldiers about six kilometers long military convoys entered Baghdad. While the occupation almost filled the first month, the Firdevs square incident broke out. On April 9, 2003, the Saddam Hussein statue erected on the Firdevs Square of Baghdad was overthrown by the heavy US military equipment. Among the few demonstrations of the Iraqi people were destroyed, the head of the statue was cut and rolled on the ground. These events symbolize the fall of the Saddam regime. The war continued till the execution of Saddam Hussein, who was captured in a shelter in Tikrit, on December 30, 2006. More than 1 million people have died in this process. People were subjected to the most severe torture and subjected to ill-treatment. The US saw every civilian as a potential criminal and massacred them with arbitrary bombings (Blaydes 2015). At the same time, the United States has declared its name by the systematic torture of the oppressed Iraqis near Baghdad and the actions that human dignity cannot accept. Abu Ghraib has committed many war crimes in prison. This war has initiated a new process in Iraq, as well as the chaos and occupation that has led to the instability of all these violations (Sadat 2004). One of the main factors that shaped the political structure of the country after the invasion of Iraq was sectarianism. Sunni Arabs, the dominant power of the Baathist regime, were largely excluded from the Iraqi politics in the US occupation and afterward. The Shiite Arabs, which had little influence during the Saddam era, became the dominant political power with the intense support of the US and Iran. The Sunnis and Shiites could not eliminate the tension even if they tried to come together under a secular and liberal political structures due to the lack of any power to stabilize the country (Council on Foreign Affairs 2017).

However, in the military operation of the US against Iraq, the oil issue is crucial. This is due to the US dependence on oil. The US consumes 25 % of the worldwide oil and imports half of what it consumes. In this respect, the main policy of President Bush was to meet the increasing demand for oil. According to the energy plan made in 2001, it was predicted that US oil demand would increase rapidly and that oil imports would increase from 10.4 million barrels daily to 20.7 million barrels in 2020 (Birdsall 2003, p. 60). Of the US's oil imports, 25 % are from the Middle East. The Middle East alone owns 63 % of the world's oil reserves. Iraq is the third largest oil country after Saudi Arabia and Iran, with a 10 percent share of 115 billion barrels of proven oil reserves. It is thought that this figure could reach around 300 billion dollars by new researches. On the other hand, the fact that the cost of oil production in Iraq is well below the world average raises profit rates. The economic stagnation of the US and the depreciation of the US in 2001 led to the appreciation of the Euro in some countries, especially China. During this period, after 1999, the indexing of Iraq to the Euro instead of the dollar in the international sales of oil brought about the argument that the dollar could undermine the feature of being the key currency in the international market (Fratzscher 2009, p. 23). In the 2003 invasion of Iraq, these economic reasons and regime change debates are not to be overlooked. It is claimed that Iraq has an effect on the dollar's domination over oil, especially on the new conservatives in America, which has an end to the invasion of Iraq (Clark 2005).

EU's Iraq Policy and Ineffectiveness in Iraqi Intervention: A Bee That Cannot Make Honey

After the 9/11 attacks, the differences in EU and US policies have strained relations between the two sides. The EU's understanding of terrorism, soft power, peace-building, political, and economic restructuring and the US's traditional use of force and war against terrorism have revealed the fundamental distinction between the actors (Dudouet 2011, p. 10).

Differences of opinion among EU countries over an Iraqi intervention have not only prevented unilateral action over the matter but also adversely affected the relations between the US and the EU (Kagan 2004). In a meeting held at the

EU Security Institute in March 2003, disagreements about the intervention were discussed over a number of sessions. Firstly, the Bush government believed that weapons of mass destruction held by Iraq posed a threat to their national security, while European states argued that threat posed by these weapons could be controlled. Secondly, EU member states demanded that the use of force against Iraq should comply with the UN Security Council resolution, while the United States countered the demand by arguing that its actions were prompted by self-defense. Third, while the European states focused exclusively on the intervention in Iraq, the United States considered the intervention from a broader perspective—as an intervention in the Middle East (Byman and Waxman 2000, p. 87). Both NATO and EU members strongly debated the military intervention in Iraq before its occupation. This has not only strained the relations between the EU and the US but also led to a disagreement among EU member states.

The US has argued that Saddam's regime is linked to al-Qaeda, and that intervention in Iraq is part of the fight against international terrorism. However, the US has also provided justification for the war in Iraq as a weapon of mass destruction, threatened by neighboring countries. These reasons far from satisfied the public, nor could they convince EU member states of the intervention. For this reason, EU member states such as Germany, Belgium, Luxembourg, and France opposed US intervention in Iraq (McNeill 2018, p. 8). Donald Rumsfeld called the group of these states as Old Europe (Hooper and Black 2003).

However, the UK, one of the most important countries of the EU, has seen its future next to the US, but not the EU. In this sense, instead of acting in solidarity with EU countries, and acting on a monophonic structure within the scope of the EU's Common Foreign and Security Policy, the UK has taken its place and has given full support to the Bush administration (Hooper and Black 2003).

According to the declaration, which was published in various sources in Europe on January 31, 2003, and known as the Letter of Eight, eight European states stated that they were in solidarity with the US. This text, known as Europe and the United States Must Be Together, signed by Britain, Spain, Italy, Portugal, Czech Republic, Hungary, Poland, and Denmark, states that democracy, personal freedoms, human rights, and fundamental values were born in Europe and transcended the Atlantic to operate in European institutions. The text, which says that the 9/11 attacks were an attack on these fundamental values, says that the European and American union is a guarantee of freedom. The Eight, who expressed that the US saved Europe from the Nazis and the Communists in the twentieth century, emphasized that the weapons of mass destruction of Iraq posed a major threat, and that this threat would end with a common struggle to be carried out together (Lewis 2008, p. 30). Moreover, the Eight said that opposing this intervention meant the fragmentation of the EU's common foreign and security policy. In contrast, European states opposing the intervention have dealt with the lack of an alternative policy.

Actually, the reason for their opposition to the Iraqi intervention was related to the concern about the deterioration of the environment of trust and order in Iraq after the intervention. According to this, Iraq was worried about internal turmoil after the intervention, which consisted of different ethnic and sectarian structures, and was governed by an authoritarian regime for a long time. On the other hand, the states that opposed the intervention requested that they should act in accordance with the principle of multilateralism in the framework of UN principles by opposing the unilateral movement of the US. They claim that there is no definitive evidence that there is a weapon of mass destruction in Iraq (Menon 2004, p. 634). The fact that European states highlight their own national policies rather than acting on a common foreign policy led to the failure of the European Union (Ortaga 2008, p. 27). For example, after the 2003 Iraqi intervention, in order to provide post-war security in Iraq, 15000 troops were sent from Britain and the Eight sent 5,000 troops. Germany and France, who opposed the intervention, did not send troops. This situation prevented the European Union from producing a more active and powerful policy on Iraq (Youngs 2004, p. 8).

According to the member states of the EU, the definition of common threat was needed during the crisis in order to correct the disagreements caused by the invasion of Iraq. To this end, Javier Solana, the High Commissioner for the Common Foreign and Security Policy of the EU, was appointed on April 2003; it was unanimously decided that, as a result of Sweden's initiatives, a common opinion on the dissemination of weapons of mass destruction in the European Union would be determined (Mix 2013, p. 22).

Nevertheless, the vast majority of European states have not ratified the US policy and intervention in Iraq. Instead, the EU has pursued a policy of balancing the US on Iraq policy. In this way, the EU has had to redefine itself. The draft text of the European Security Strategy plan presented by Solana at the EU's Thessaloniki summit was discussed in June 2003 (European Commission 2003). In the European Security Strategy, which came into force on December 12, 2003, the European Union changed both threat perception and traditional interests. The European Security Strategy document set forth at the summit hinted that the EU is a candidate for an ambitious foreign policy. The EU, for the first time, took into account the international security environment with the European Security Strategy, and the future foreign policy objectives and instruments were determined. According to this document, the EU's main threat points are global terrorism, the spread of weapons of mass destruction and decadent regimes (European Union 2003).

Accordingly, global terrorism has been recognized as a strategic threat to the EU. It was also stated in the document that it was not a possibility for terrorists to use weapons of mass destruction. In the document, which sees the proliferation of weapons of mass destruction as a priority threat to the EU, it is seen as a significant threat that the states in the Middle East region obtain these weapons. However, the declining regimes have been seen as the reason for the EU to be the target of migration and organized crime. Therefore, it was stated that the situation of these states should be improved (European Commission 2003).

In this process, the EU institutions could not agree on any other issue except to defend the implementation of UN resolutions open to different interpretations. The result is a complete 'disappointment for the EU's goal of developing common and effective policies against international problems. The EU, which is an economic giant military and political dwarf, who wants to be a global power, but has not succeeded in this sense, has not been able to develop an active and monolithic policy during the Iraq intervention through a bee that cannot make honey due to its institutional structure and decision-making mechanism. After the war, the EU tried to contribute to the recovery of Iraq as soon as possible by using the soft power of the member countries (Walt 2013).

Conclusion

The 9/11 attacks have been one of the important turning points that have changed the political history of the world. The attacks on US strategic areas have led to a change in US foreign policy and security strategies, as well as bringing together actors involved in the international system in combating terrorism. After the attacks, the United States emphasized the need to tackle global terrorism and declared war against terrorism and hostile states. In this context, al-Qaeda leader Osama Bin Laden and his supporter have intervened in Afghanistan. After the intervention in Afghanistan, he intervened in Iraq on March 20, 2003, and overthrew the Saddam Hussein regime on the grounds that Hussein produced a weapon of mass destruction and supported terrorism.

The US did not find any weapons of mass destruction in the course of the nine years of occupation. While he was rapidly losing power in the region with the heavily-armed forces in the clashes he had with the local armed forces, he withdrew all of his troops stationed in Iraq. With the chaos experienced, many Iraqis had a hard time because of the war trauma, and many of them committed suicide. More than 1 million people have been massacred, and rape and torture in the region have become part of everyday life. The US is now written with a black mark in the pages of history due to both this failed state and the massacres and rape.

In this process, the EU primarily condemned terrorism. However, there was no single-voice and common policy of the EU in subsequent events. The EU has failed to make an expected move due to its institutional structure and decision-making mechanism, and disagreements between member states have hampered a more active policy. The EU, considered to be an economic giant but a political and military dwarf, is far from its goal of becoming a global power because it cannot produce as effective a policy as it wishes due to its decision-making and institutional structure. This has also been seen in the political moves during the Iraqi intervention. For this reason, it should show its power in a military and political manner in an institutional and decision-making structure. In this way, the EU, with its bold steps in foreign policy and security, will be able to contribute to intellectual change in which America will accept itself as a global actor. Moreover, the European states can only gain the ambition and motivation they have not lost together.

The fact that the EU is not so important in strategic matters so far is not due to the lack of military capacity and the lack of the common political will to use such power. The main obstacles to the EU's failure to be an international actor are the insufficiency of military power in crisis management, the lack of political will among the member states, and the lack of effective institutional mechanisms.

The Iraq War process has led to some important decisions to be taken to address the shortcomings of the Common Foreign and Security Policy and to eliminate them. One of the important consequences of the interrogation process was the fact that the EU could contribute to an international crisis like Iraq by not using its military power but by using its civil power. In this context, the spread of democracy worldwide from the regions close to Europe has been adopted as a key objective for the Common Foreign and Security Policy. In this context, the use of tools such as transferring the experience of state administration, assisting in the development of democratic institutions, economic and humanitarian aid, and the development of commercial relations and regional cooperation are taken as the basis.

The European Union, with its political/military-dominated international problems like the 2003 Iraqi Crisis, at least aiming to stand out with its civil forces, is aware of the difficulty of developing a common foreign policy with political and military means, at least at the level of political integration that the EU has reached. The EU members, who have a common interest in the Middle East in general and Iraq in particular, wanted to be effective on developments in the region and country by following a common policy after the war. In this respect, the EU has sought to contribute to the reconstruction of Iraq by focusing on areas such as the realization of the rule of law and the realization of human rights, democratization, the functioning of the basic public services expected by citizens, and humanitarian aid. However, if the EU wants to be a global power, it should have a single voice structure by solving the disruption in the structure of decision-making. It would be in the best interest of the EU to ensure this structure. In this way, the EU will be able to increase its power from military and political weaknesses. However, if the deficiencies cannot be eliminated through the partial consolidation of the Common Foreign and Security Policy, the EU appears to be doomed to remain as an actor, partial or incomplete in the most optimistic definition.

References

American Rhetoric: *Address to the Nation on the Threat of Iraq*, retrieved 11.01.2019 from, https://www.americanrhetoric.com/speeches/gwbushwariniraqcincinnati.htm.

Bennett, Christopher: *Combating Terrorism. NATO Review*, retrieved 09.01.2018 from, https://www.nato.int/docu/review/2003/issue1/english/art2.html.

Biddle, Stephan D: *American Grand Strategy after 9/11: An Assessment*. PA: U.S. Army War College Strategic Studies, 2005.

Birdsall, Nancy: "The Real Challenge for Iraqi Development". *The International Economy* 17 (8), 2003, Fall, pp. 58–61.

Blaydes, Lisa: *Compliance and Resistance in Iraq under Saddam Hussein*, retrieved 07.01.2019 from, http://cpd.berkeley.edu/wp-content/uploads/2015/03/ComplianceResistanceFeb2015.pdf.

Byman, Daniel and Waxman, Matthew: *Confronting Iraq: U.S. Policy and the Use of Force since the Gulf War*. Santa Monica: Rand, 2000.

CIA: *National Strategy for Combating Terrorism*, retrieved 05.01.2019 from, https://www.cia.gov/news-information/cia-the-war-on-terrorism/Counter_Terrorism_Strategy.pdf.

Clark, Willism: *Petrodollar Warfare: Dollars, Euros and the Upcoming Iranian Oil Bourse*, retrieved 03.01.2019 from, https://www.resilience.org/stories/2005-08-08/petrodollar-warfare-dollars-euros-and-upcoming-iranian-oil-bourse/.

CNN: *Bush Gives an Update on the War against Terrorism*, retrieved 02.01.2019 from, http://edition.cnn.com/2001/US/10/11/gen.bush.transcript/.

Coats, Daniel R: *Statement for the Record: Worldwide Threat Assessment of the US Intelligence Community*. PA: Director of National Intelligence, 2018.

Council on Foreign Affairs: *The Global Regime for Terrorism*, retrieved 31.12.2018 from, https://www.cfr.org/report/global-regime-terrorism.

Council on Foreign Affairs: *The Sunni-Shia Divide*, retrieved 21.12.2018 from, https://www.cfr.org/interactives/sunni-shia-divide#!/sunni-shia-divide.

Cox, Michael: "Paradigm Shifts and 9/11: International Relations after the Twin Towers". *Security Dialogue* 33 (2), 2002, pp. 247–251.

Dudouet, Veronique: "Anti-Terrorism Legislation: Impediments to Conflict Transformation". *Berghof Policy Brief* (2), 2011, pp. 1–16.

European Commission: *Thessaloniki European Council 19 and 20 June 2003 Presidency Conclusions*, retrieved 30.12.2018 from, http://europa.eu/rapid/press-release_DOC-03-3_en.htm.

European Union: *European Security Strategy: A Secure Europe in a Better World*, retrieved 29.12.2018 from, https://europa.eu/globalstrategy/en/european-security-strategy-secure-europe-better-world.

Fratzscher, Marcel: "What Explains Global Exchange Rate Movements during the Financial Crisis". *European Central Bank Working Paper Series* (1060), 2009, pp. 1–44.

Gohel, Sajjan M: "Deciphering Ayman Al-Zawahiri and Al-Qaeda's Strategic and Ideological Imperatives". *Perspectives on Terrorism* 11 (1), 2017, pp. 54–67.

Hooper, John and Black, Ian: *Anger at Rumsfeld Attack on Old Europe*, retrieved 26.12.2018 from, https://www.theguardian.com/world/2003/jan/24/germany.france.

House of Representative: *Provıde Appropriate Tools Requıred to Intercept and Obstruct Terrorısm (Patrıot) Act of 2001*, retrieved 25.12.2018 from, https://www.gpo.gov/fdsys/pkg/CRPT-107hrpt236/pdf/CRPT-107hrpt236-pt1.pdf.

Hulse, Carl and Mitchell, Allison: *Threats and Responses: The Vote; Congress Authorızes Bush to Use Force Agaınst Iraq Use Force Agaınst Iraq, Creatıng a Broad Mandate*, retrieved 23.12.2018 from, https://www.nytimes.com/2002/10/11/us/threats-responses-vote-congress-authorizes-bush-use-force-against-iraq-creating.html.

Jenkins, Brian: "The Organization Men Anatomy of a Terrorist Attack". In: J. f. Rose (Ed). *How Did This Happen: Terrorism and the New War*. New York: Public Affairs, 2001, pp. 1–14.

Kagan, Robert: *America's Crisis of Legitimacy*, retrieved 15.05.2019 from, https://www.foreignaffairs.com/articles/united-states/2004-03-01/americas-crisis-legitimacy.

Leading to War: *Bush Administration Claims vs. Facts*, retrieved 20.12.2018 from, http://www.leadingtowar.com/claims_facts_iraqnotinvolved.php.

Leffler, Melvyn P: "9/11 and the Past and Future of American Foreign Policy". *Royal Institute of International Affairs* 79 (5), 2003, pp. 1045–1063.

Lewis, Jeffrey: *EU Policy in Iraq: The Collapse and Reconstruction of Consensus-Based Foreign Policy*. Dublin: Dublin European Institute, 2008.

Lindstrom, Gustav: "Terrorism: European Myths and Realities". In: G. Lindstrom (Ed). *Shift or Rift: Assessing US-EU Relations after Iraq*. Paris: Institute for Security Studies, 2003, pp. 231–250.

McNeill, Daniel: "Why Was Iraq Invaded in 2003?" *Upgraduate Journal of Politics and International Relations* 1 (1), 2018, pp. 1–16.

Menon, Anand: "From Crisis to Catharsis: ESDP after Iraq". *International Affairs* 80 (4), 2004, pp. 631–648.

Mix, Derek E: "The European Union: Foreign and Security Policy". *CRS Report* (41959), 2013, pp. 1–29.

North, Bill and Vann, David: *Bush Speaks at West Point: From Containment to "Rollback"*, retrieved 19.12.2018 from, https://www.wsws.org/en/articles/2002/06/bush-j04.htm.

Oltermann, Philip: *Can Europe's New Xenophobes Reshape the Continent?* retrieved 18.12.2018 from, https://www.theguardian.com/world/2018/feb/03/europe-xenophobes-continent-poland-hungary-austria-nationalism-migrants.

Ortaga, Martin: "Iraq: A European Point of View". *The European Union Institute for Security Studies Occasional Paper* (40), 2008, pp. 1–34.

Pan, Esther: *Iraq: Justifying the War*, retrieved 19.12.2018 from, https://www.cfr.org/backgrounder/iraq-justifying-war.

Rosand, Eric: "The Security Council as "Global Legislator": Ultra Vires or Ultra Innovative?". *Fordham International Law Journal* 28 (3), 2004, p. 542–590.

Sadat, L. Nadia: *International Legal Issues Surrounding the Mistreatment of Iraqi Detainees by American Forces*, retrieved 17.12.2018 from, https://www.tjsl.edu/slomansonb/AbuGhraib.pdf.

Santos, Maria Helena De Castro and Teixeria, Ulysses Tavares, "The Essential Role of Democracy in the Bush Doctrine: The Invasions of Iraq and Afghanistan". *Rev. Bras. Polít. Int* 56 (2), 2013, pp. 131–156.

Smyrl, Marc: European Anti-Terrorism Policy: a Trans-Atlantic Perspective. *Politique européenne* (23), 2007, pp. 115–132.

Spencer, Alexander: "Questioning the Concept of 'New Terrorism". *Peace Conflict and Development* (8), 2006, pp. 1–33.

Teather, David: *Civil Libertarians Prepare to Fight Bush over Tougher Anti-Terror Laws*, retrieved 17.12.2018 from, https://www.theguardian.com/

uk-news/2015/jan/12/david-cameron-pledges-anti-terror-law-internet-paris-attacks-nick-clegg.

The British Prime Minister: *Responsıbılıty for the Terrorıst Atrocıtıes in the Unıted States, 11 September 2001 - An Updated Account*, retrieved 14.12.2018 from, https://fas.org/irp/news/2001/11/ukreport.html.

The Guardian: *Bush: Saddam Was Not Responsible for 9/11*, retrieved 15.12.2018 from, https://www.theguardian.com/world/2006/sep/12/september11.US.

The Guardian: *The Text of George Bush's Speech*, retrieved 13.12.2018 from, https://www.theguardian.com/world/2001/sep/21/september11US13.

The Washington Post: *Text: President Bush Addresses the Nation*, retrieved 10.12.2018 from, http://www.washingtonpost.com/wp-srv/nation/specials/attacked/transcripts/bushaddress_092001.html?noredirect=on

The White House: *Selected Speeches of President George W. Bush 2001–2008*, retrieved 10.12.2018 from, https://georgewbush-whitehouse.archives.gov/infocus/bushrecord/documents/Selected_Speeches_George_W_Bush.pdf.

The White House: *The National Strategy of the United States of America*. Washington: The White House, 2002.

Thrall, A. Trevor, and Goepner, Eric: "Step Back: Lessons for U.S. Foreign Policy from the Failed War on Terror". *CATO Institute Policy Paper* (814), 2017, pp. 1–42.

United Nations: *Statement by President Bush United Nations General Assembly, UN Headquarters, New York 12 September 2002*, retrieved 12.03.2019 from, http://www.un.org/webcast/ga/57/statements/020912USE.htm.

United Nations General Assembly: *Condemnation of the Terrorist Attacks in the United States of America*, retrieved 13.03.2019 from, http://www.un.org/documents/ga/docs/56/agresolution.htm.

United Nations Security Council: *Resolution 1368 (2001) Adopted by the Security Council at Its 4370th Meeting on*, retrieved 10.12.2018 from, http://www.un.org/en/ga/search/view_doc.asp?symbol=S/RES/1368%20%282001%29.

United Nations Security Council: *Resolution 1373*, retrieved 15.03.2019 from, http://www.un.org/en/ga/search/view_doc.asp?symbol=S/RES/1373%20%282001%29.

United Nations Security Council: *Resolution 1441 (2002) Adopted by the Security Council at Its 4644th Meeting, on 8 November 2002*, retrieved 15.3.2019 from, http://www.un.org/Depts/unmovic/documents/1441.pdf.

United States Army Reserve: *The Indispensable Force: The Post Cold War Operational Army Reserve 1990–2010*. Washington: USRC, 2013.

Walt, Stephen: *Iran Is the Main Beneficiary of the Iraq War*, retrieved 22.12.2018 from, https://www.theeuropean-magazine.com/stephen-walt--3/6617-ten-years-after-the-iraq-invasion.

White Paper: "9/11: A Brief History and a Case Study of America's Worst Terrorist Attacks". *SAC LSUS Report* (10), 2016, pp. 1–269.

Youngs, Richard: "Europe and Iraq from Standoff to Engagement?" *Center for European Policy Studies Working Document* (216), 2004, pp. 1–14.

İdris TURAN

II The 1990–1991 Gulf Crisis from a Neorealist Perspective

Abstract: In this study, the neorealist approach is tested by means of the case study starting with the 1990 Gulf Crisis and resulting in the war of 1991 due to creating imbalance in the international system. In light of the basic arguments of neorealism, it is put forward by this case study what can happen in the event of a crisis unbalancing the international system. In general terms, it is observed by the case study that the international system dominates world politics. This study elaborates on neorealist arguments within the framework of the Gulf Crisis and its repercussions.

Keywords: 1990–1991 Gulf Crisis, Neorealism, the US, Iraq, Kuwait

Introduction

The Gulf Crisis emerged after the end of the Cold War and function as a litmus paper for the structure of the international system and the powers dominating the international system (primarily the US – United States). It is deemed suitable to explain this crisis where the international system comes to the fore through neorealist arguments. As a matter of fact, neorealism propounded by Kenneth Waltz argues that the international system is determinative for actors. The Gulf Crisis is one that has repercussions on Asia, the Middle East, Europe, and the American continent. Kuwait has great importance for the international system. It is for this reason that the repercussions of the crisis were observed in such a large geography.

This crisis is also significant in terms of revealing the effect of the US on the UN (United Nations), the organization bringing legitimacy to various steps to be taken in the international system. On the other hand, it is shown that Russia has been lagging behind in affecting the international system and the UN.

The purpose of this study is to test the neorealist approach on the basis of the 1990–1991 Gulf Crisis. The assumption of the study is that if a state has material power and opts for extending its borders and sphere of influence against the system, this expansion effort will be prevented by various mechanisms since it will threaten the balance in the system. Indeed, the invasion of Kuwait by Iraq paved the way for an international crisis, and the Gulf Crisis was quenched by a military intervention led by the powers dominating the system.

Neorealism and the Crisis Situation

According to realism, what is important in international relations is to protect the balance of power. Great powers are basic actors in the system. States pay attention to the status of their relative economic and military power. The systemic balance depends on the power of other states not exceeding the level where they can change the system. In neorealism, put forward by Kenneth Waltz, on the other hand, not actors (states), but the international system is determinative.

Neorealism (structural realism) has five basic theoretical assumptions (Mearsheimer 2013, pp. 77–93):

- Great powers are the main actors of world politics and they act in an anarchic – lack of supreme authority – system.
- Every state has material power with a possibility to show aggression against another state at a certain level.
- States may never be sure about the intentions of other states.

States aspire to know whether a state is revisionist – implementing policies to change the system – or *status quo* supporter – implementing policies to preserve the current system. Contrary to military capacity, however, intentions cannot be measured and therefore, precision about state intentions are mostly impossible. Even though it is possible to make inferences from statements of statesmen or official documents, surety is not possible whether these statements reflect the real intentions or not. The fundamental purpose of states is to survive. States strive to protect their *territorial integrity* and maintain their autonomy in local policies.

- States are *rational* actors. This rationality means generating policies to increase the potential of survival.

Due to not being sure about each other's intentions and feeling insecure, states develop *self-help* strategies and apply policies in this line. They operate to become more powerful. Once a state acts in this line, other states will also adopt this attitude leading to triggering reciprocal power-up initiatives, which ultimately results in the emergence of what is called the *security dilemma* (Mearsheimer 2013, pp. 77–93). Tension caused by the security dilemma sometimes evolves into wars.

There is no single impetus for reasons of wars according to neorealism. The act of war emerges through a combination of multiple factors. These factors are as follows (Mearsheimer 2013, pp. 77–93):

- Polarization of the system (unipolar, bipolar, and multipolar),
- The situation with regard to balancing the powers,
- Power distribution,
- The balance between defense and attack.

Conceptualization of the Neorealist Approach

Relational power (transactional power or *bargaining power* as defined by Krause) is used to refer to create pressure on those who demand a value/meta by those who own this value or meta. In the literature of international relations, on the other hand, it means relational gaining of a dependent state (*client state*) from the state it depends on (*patron state*). Structural power, on the other hand, is used by a leading state in mid-term. It creates a driving force for leading states to achieve their targets. Other states than the leading states, on the other hand, respond in order to reduce or eliminate their dependence or vulnerability. Between relational/bargaining power and structural power, there is a hegemonic power that is not directly observed, but functions at a different level. In cases where this power is apparent, the aim of the leading state is not to cooperate with a non-leading state for a specific or situational subject, but to ensure that this state abides by the rules of security and threat established by the leading state (Sözen 2010).

The security dilemma, according to Glaser, has the tendency to become harder either when defensive states has an advantage against aggressive states or at times when defensive and aggressive strategies are not distinguishable (Lawson 2001).

Glaser underlines that there is a close relationship between policy-making instruments and policies that states implement in crises. Specifically, military organizations and interest groups may acquire extensive gains by exaggerating the counter party's aggressive power and alleging that they have malicious intentions even though their defensive powers are ambiguous in purpose (Lawson 2001).

Despite various areas of usage, *balancing* generally indicates alliance with other states against a more powerful or threatening force/coalition; and the following *bandwagoning*, on the other hand, points out to participation to a more powerful organization/entity. Although they have difference in their arguments, all leading realist scholars including Kenneth Waltz, Stephen Walt, and John Mearsheimer utter that states prefer balancing over bandwagoning (Rhodes 2004).

Bridging, on the other hand, refers to efforts of mediation between two different powers or blocks with a purpose of developing relations. Rather than being against any of such parties, this act is about increasing cooperation between both parties or minimizing conflicts between them (Rhodes 2004).

Hegemony is commonly regarded as structural. Hegemonic states pave the way for their interests and consolidate their dominance by shaping the socio-economic or ideological environment (Cooper, Higgot, and Nossal 1991). Even though a collective security system is right or wrong, it is designed in a way to fulfill the hegemonic desires of hegemonic states (Hunter 1990). Super powers look after their interests and provide assistance to other states in a way that will not disturb the existing balance (Hartung 1990).

The relationship between leading and dependent states (*clientelism*) is a strategic relationship between weak and powerful states. While leading states (*patron*) wish to launch the strategic goods and services in dependent states (*clients*) to the market, they also provide security to dependent states in order to ensure continuity. The United Kingdom was a leading state for Kuwait in the nineteenth century (Tétreault 1991). The United Kingdom left its leadership of the region to the US after the World War II.

Another argument in neorealism is that the anarchic world lacking a supreme authority is a world full of threats. Members of this chronically perilous world must act to prevent aggression that may erupt anywhere (Brown 1991).

Assumptions of the neorealist approach can be summarized in three articles. The first of these is anarchy, which is the regulatory principle of the international system (absence of a supreme authority), the second is the behavioral pattern of states to prioritize security, which makes states resemble each other, and the third is the power distribution which determines the positions of actors in the system. This power distribution determines the behaviors of the actors in the international system. These three arguments are the ones that paved the way for the emergence of neorealism.

In light of this information, this study explains the international and regional situation in the 1990s, the circumstances under which Iraq wanted to implement revisionist policies, the counter reactions of Kuwait to protect its territorial integrity and the reasons for the war (coalition intervention). Consequently, an evaluation is made on the basis of the ramifications of the crisis and the war.

International and Regional Environment between 1990 and 1991

A power gap emerged together with the disintegration of the USSR (Union of Soviet Socialist Republics) after the Cold War. This power gap strengthened the unipolar position of the US, increased the security needs of the US, and made the world more vulnerable to US interventions. The role of the US in this period is evaluated as "the sole power to shape the peaceful world" (Walker 1990).

In the 1980s, the presence of Egypt in the Arab region as well as the regional balance was upset by the fact that Egypt and Saudi Arabia shifted their axis towards the Western Block and Egypt signed a peace agreement* with Israel in 1979 after the Camp David negotiations (Sayigh 1991). After gaining an advantage over Iran as a result of the war, Iraq reached the position of a leader in the region also with the effect of its strategic location for the Gulf Region and the Eastern Mediterranean (Sayigh 1991). During the course of the war with Iran, Baathist-secular Saddam Hossein (Head 2013) increased his military influence on the region with the support of the West and the Soviet Union.

The consequences of the disintegration of the Soviet Union became an important factor in upsetting regional balance and leading to an overall crisis in the states located in the Arab geography (Sayigh 1991). The Israeli airstrike on Iraq's nuclear reactor in 1981 (Brands 2011) was responded positively by Washington and this caused Saddam Hossein, as the previous Iraqi leaders, to bear enmity against Israel. Furthermore, he considered that this policy of enmity would enable him to become the leader of the Arab world (Springborg 1990). This attitude by Saddam was responded by suspicion and disturbance by the US and Israel and therefore, Saddam was classified as a threat to the New World Order emerging after the Cold War with the incrementing interest in human rights (Springborg 1990). On the other hand, Saddam felt growingly insecure due to his fears of conspiracy by Israel and the US (Brands 2011).

Iraq and Kuwait

A relatively isolated city-state, Kuwait comes forward as a mercantile port for the Arabian Peninsula (Tétreault 1991). Indeed, Kuwait was an annexed region to Iraq in 1899. However, the British created a protectorate with the help of the local Kuwaitis and aimed to use the harbor reaches and petroleum reserves there in their favor by supporting the Kuwaitis to become a separate nation (Head 2013).

Looking from the perspective of the historical background of the relations between Iraq and Kuwait, it can be seen that Iraq threatened Kuwait two times in 1961. It seized the north of Kuwait between the years 1973 and 1974 (Tétreault 2000), and withdrew with the counter attack of Kuwait in 1975 under the Soviet pressure (Tétreault 1991). It is stated that there are two main factors which drove Iraq to target Kuwait: The claim that Kuwait stole petroleum from Iraq

---

* * Egypt's siding with Israel through a peace agreement had a negative effect on its aspiration for Arab leadership and paved the way for Iraq to come forward in the Arab world.

and did not give two strategic islands – Bubiyan and Warba – to reach the Gulf (Hunter 1990).

The Iraqi attack on Iran was underlined to be a serious threat against world peace according to the Charter of the United Nations. Nonetheless, the UN did not take any initiative to stop this attack (Hunter 1990). When Kuwait was invaded, on the other hand, the international system showed reaction and the UN issued a decision to intervene.

During the oil crisis between 1973 and 1979, the high importance of the Gulf region – in terms of its place and size in the global economy – was realized (Overseas Development Institute 1991). The 1990 Gulf Crisis broke out in the Middle Eastern region with the highest amount of oil reserves. As it can be seen in the resolutions of the Security Council, states came together to form an alliance against Iraq in order to overcome this crisis outbreaking in the Gulf region.

Implementation of Revisionist Strategies by Iraq

Iraq exhibited a strong image with high military capacity in the region during the 8-year war against the Islamic Republic of Iran (Lawson 2001). The Baghdad administration deemed itself as the protector or patron of the Arab nation and as a shield against non-Arabs – Persians and other external threats (Korany 1990). During the war with Iran, Baghdad obtained financial support from the Gulf countries, while acquiring advanced-technology arms from the Western states and the Soviet Union (Stein 1992). During the war between Iraq and Iran, the US provided Iraq with limited support in a way to prevent the country to gain a hegemonic position in the Gulf region (Maat 2011).

It was stated that Saddam needed to eliminate the barriers in order to become a modern Selahattin (Stein 1990). For this, he needed to control oil shipment, and ensure that Iraq rose as a dominant actor in the regional and international system. In line with this target, Iraq first fought against its competitor, Iran and then invaded Kuwait** trusting its military capacity despite the acute economic crisis in the country (Lawson 2001).

In the process evolving into the invasion of Kuwait, first a crisis broke out between Iraq and the Arab States, while the statement of the Iraqi Minister of Oil on May 1 through the Baghdad Radio saying "OPEC (*Organization of Petroleum Exporting Countries*) were subject to being dependent on an oil quota" became the first signal of the incoming crisis (Springborg 1990). In May 1990, Saddam

* The US initiatives to direct Saddam to invade Kuwait are significant in the process that led to this invasion by Iraq.

Hossein accused the administrations of the Arab states in the Gulf region of sabotaging the Iraqi economy by keeping oil prices artificially low (Stein 1990).

On July 16, 1990, the Minister of Foreign Affairs Tarık Aziz notified Kuwait about the following issues with the demand of Saddam: The Minister demanded 2.4 billion dollars from Kuwait due to the reason that Kuwait profits from the contradictive Rumelia petroleum field and another 12 billion dollars with the assertion that Kuwait played with oil prices against Iraq. Furthermore, he demanded Kuwait to pay its debt of 10 billion dollars borrowed during the war between Iraq and Iran. In addition to all these, he states that Kuwait needed to withdraw from the Island of Bubiyan, the one and only Iraqi port which enables control over access to Umm Qasr (Stein 1990). On July 17, 1990 – the 22nd anniversary of Baath Party's coming to power, Saddam Hussein blamed the Gulf countries to intentionally keep oil prices low via excessive production by falling under the effect of the US (Springborg 1990). Before submitting evidence to the Senate's Committee of Foreign Affairs, the US Ambassador April C. Glaspie (http://www.nytimes.com 1991) issued a serious verbal stern warning against Saddam indicating that force would be used against him (Stein 1990).

Kuwaiti Minister of Interior Sheikh Salim el-Sabah claimed before the war that they could trust the US (Stein 1990). Due to its leader-dependent relationship, Kuwait was aware of its importance in the international system and had a rational idea* purporting that this importance would form a shield for the country.

The Importance of Kuwait for the System

As much as all other states of the world dependent on the Middle Eastern oil, the Gulf Crisis had a negative impact on the South Asian countries and their relations with the Gulf countries in economic and political terms (Malik 1991).

For instance, India was importing 40 % of its oil from Iraq and Kuwait. In addition, India had 185 thousand of its citizens working in these countries. As a secular state, Iraq was a traditionally friendly nation to India and supported India in the Kashmir Issue (Malik 1991). However, India started to feel the negative economic effects of the crisis in the region in a short while. Despite the Iraqi support to India in the Kashmir Issue, India sided with the coalition powers.

The Japanese government was torn between the desires of the US as its ally and its policy of traditionally maintaining amicable relations with Arabs in order

---

* Being aware of its position in the international system, Kuwait was rescued from Iraq by the coalition powers under the US leadership.

to ensure stable oil importation (Purrington and K. 1991). Due to its energy dependence, Japan declared that it would provide economic support to the intervention three weeks after the US notified its demands on August 29, 1990 (Purrington and K. 1991).

An important factor that made the US policy complicated in the Gulf region was that the Bush administration was not an independent actor *(free agent)* anymore. Any military decision started to require an extensive negotiation process and if possible, taking permission/issuing resolution from the UNSC (United Nations Security Council) (Walker 1990). The reason for this is that the UN needed a strategy after the disintegration of the USSR to maintain its position of world leadership over other states with minimum harm/cost by using the fundamental norms of the UN.

The Reaction of the International System Against the Invasion of Kuwait

According to Glaser, there are two reasons behind state motivations to expand: To expand and increase their security by means of using advantages in an insecure environment (Lawson 2001). For this reason, Iraq wanted to implement its strategies over Kuwait which was relatively less powerful than itself. Accusing Kuwait for Iraq's economic crisis, Saddam attacked Kuwait by thinking that the balance of power was in favor of Iraq.

The military power of Iraq in 1990 was as follows: 1 million soldiers, 5500 offense tanks, 1000 armored vehicles, 3700 cannons, 160 gunships, approximately 500 tactical assault aircrafts, 1500 air defense gantries, and near 4000–6000 antiaircraft weapons. Iraq was the world's fifth largest military power in that period (Cordesman 2001). Furthermore, 1000 medium-range al-Hüseyin and long-range al-Abbas missiles were available in the Iraqi army in the spring of 1990 (Lawson 2001).

Saddam made an announcement through the Baghdad Radio saying, "For those who oppose to them, Iraq and Kuwait would be a graveyard" (CBC/Radio-Canada 1990) and on August 2, 1990, at 02.00 towards the morning, the Iraqi Republican Guards of 80,000 soldiers attacked Kuwait.

The invasion of Kuwait by Iraq was protested by almost all nation-states and caused emergency alarm in the European continent and many other countries of the world. This act by Iraq violated one of the most important international norms and international legal principles: The principle of not attacking and not violating a territory under the control of a sovereign state (Sözen 2010). The violation of this norm – on which the system is established – was naturally responded by reaction in the international system.

According to the assumption of relational or bargaining power, since Kuwait has natural resources and is under protection of great powers – primarily the United Kingdom and the US – the aforementioned great powers use the opportunities to affect/direct the use of its natural resources and distribute them in line with their interests. Therefore, this state of protection by the great powers brought along political and military reaction against the invasion of Kuwait.

On July 24, 1990, Pentagon's spokesperson Pete Williams provided a statement on behalf of the US that they would ensure individual and collective security of those who they had close relations in the Gulf countries which the US had deep and long-term connections (Stein 1990). After three days, on July 27, the US Senate voting resulted in the decision to prevent Iraq from receiving loans and purchasing US-made products with 83 affirmative votes and 12 negative votes (Springborg 1990).

According to President Bush's statement on August 8, the four points in the resolution to be taken at the UN Security Council were as follows:

- Complete withdrawal of Iraq from Kuwait urgently and without any preconditions
- Restoration of the legitimate government of Kuwait
- Protection of the American citizens abroad
- The crucial importance of ensuring security and stability in the region for the national interests of the US

International observers regarded the invasion of Kuwait by Iraq as an intervention against a small and weak state (Hunter 1990). Referring to the situation of threatening peace in Chapter 7 of the Charter of the UN, the Security council took the resolution number 660. In this process, though, the efforts to ensure withdrawal of Iraq from Kuwait failed to produce any positive result. Therewith, the resolution number 678 was taken imposing that Iraq should have withdrawn until January 16, 1991, otherwise the resolution number 660 would be put into force.

In August 1990, the US feared that Iraq would shift the deployment of its forces from Kuwait to Saudi Arabia, which was an important regional ally of the US. Consequently, the US initiated the *Operation Desert Shield* and deployed its military forces in Saudi Arabia. In 35 days, the US transferred 1000 fighter jets to the region. In addition, the US planned to use these forces in the *Operation Desert Storm* in removing the Iraqi army from Kuwait (Head 2013).

In response to the international reactions, Iraq placed the condition for withdrawing from Kuwait on August 12 that Israel also must have withdrawn from the Arabic territories it had invaded. Moreover, Iraq stated that it would attack Israel if it joins the coalition against Iraq. As a matter of fact, Saddam attacked Saudi Arabia and Israel with SCUD missiles after the beginning of the airstrike by the coalition forces in January 1991. As a result of bombarding Israel with 40 missiles, 4000 buildings were damaged, and several hundreds of civilians were injured. Twenty Israeli citizens lost their lives. Saddam said through the Baghdad Radio that "Time for Arabs' victory was close, and the Zionist regime would fully pay the price for its crimes" (Brands 2011).

On November 29, 1990, the US was authorized by the UN Security Council as the leader of the coalition. According to the resolution number 678, it was projected to attack after January 15. Between January 11 and 13, 1991, American citizens were asked the question, "If Iraq does not withdraw from Kuwait until January 15, should the United States of America start a military operation against Iraq?" and 47 % responded positively. The rate of those who states the US should wait and see was 46 % (Brenner 1991).

Iraq did not abide by the decision and the coalition's air forces started to bombard Iraq on January 16, 1991. The majority of states – especially the Western Europe – agreed that Saddam should have been stopped (Brenner 1991). The US President Bush started the operation a day after the UN sent an ultimatum to Iraq to withdraw from Kuwait by saying in the oval office that, "the world cannot wait anymore" (Fairhall, Elliot and Walker 1991). Despite the airstrike, Iraq did not withdraw from Kuwait and on February 24, 1991, the coalition's land forces gathered in Saudi Arabia – primarily those who were deployed with the justification of protecting the ally – initiated the attack to ensure Iraq's withdrawal from Kuwait (Weisburd, 2004).

As of the first days of the crisis, Russia supported the UN resolutions grounded in the fact that Iraq posed the threat against the stability of the international system. Under those circumstances, Russia supported the collective and peaceful efforts of the Security Council to settle the crisis (Zenchev 1990).

At 03.00 in the night according to local time on January 17, seven states provided 668 air raid crafts and the coalition forces started the bombardment of the Iraqi army.

Consequences of the Crisis and the War

The war cost over 500 billion dollars of economic loss to Iraq. The country spent 40 % of its gross domestic product on military production (Stein 1990). At least 40 developing countries were heavily affected by the Gulf Crisis. The economic impact of the crisis on the countries was over 1 % of their gross domestic product (Overseas Development Institute 1991).

The military intervention against the invasion of Kuwait by Iraq created an opportunity long-waited by the US to establish military bases in the Gulf region

(Maat 2011). For the first time, the US deployed high numbers of land forces in the Middle East. And again, the US came at a position to fight against an Arab-Muslim nation for the first time in its history (Hunter 1990). The leadership of the US became undisputable for the first time since the World War II. The media continuously reflected this situation as "the intervention under the leadership of the US" (Cooper, Higgot and Nossal 1991).

The *United Nations Compensation Commission (UNCC)* was formed by the UN Security Council in the form of a court to investigate and clarify the international claims about the Gulf War. With the adaptation of the resolution number 687 on April 3, 1991, the UN Security Council structured the UNCC: 1) to confirm the direct losses and injuries in the state and private sector members and to affirm the responsibilities of Iraq after attacking and invading Kuwait on August 2, 1990, within the framework of the provisions of international law, 2) to create an authorized fund to cover the damages, and 3) to form the administration by the commission to manage this fund (Huth 1999).

The following consequences can be deduced from the experience of the Gulf Crisis (Brenner 1991):

- Washington carried out a UN-centered diplomacy in order to base the intervention in Iraq on the concept of "just war".
- It was proven that the US explicitly had military power.
- The effect of the US's diplomatic power in directing the coalition was understood.
- The privileged position of the US in decision-making processes within the coalition was realized. First, the US administration took the relevant decisions and then the opinions of allies were sought.
- It was proven that the allied forces showed obedience to the US leadership and even independent decisions were taken within the structural frame of the US.
- The US created a safe zone in the north of Iraq in order to ensure its interests in the region.
- The consequence for today is the fact that it is directly about national interests when great powers intervene in certain incidents, while preferring not to intervene in others.

Not any regime in the Arab world has been able to settle the chronic conflicts between Iraq and Kuwait (Tétreault 1991). This situation has been an indicator to the fact that there is not any organization/state in a hegemonic position in the region. As a matter of fact, the crisis was ultimately settled by a great power despite the initiatives of the Arab states.

Conclusion and Evaluation

The following three main conclusions can be made with regard to the 1990–1991 Gulf Crisis: Firstly, the difference in the reactions of the international system towards two different cases – in the context of the interests of a super power – is striking. In the case of the invasion of Iraq by Iran, it was not deemed necessary to refer to the fundamental principles of the UN; however, these principles were referred in the case of the invasion of Kuwait. Furthermore, there is neither UN not US intervention today in the invasion of Nagorno-Karabakh by Armenia. As it can be observed above, the US ensured issuing a resolution by the UN Security Council before attacking the Iraqi army, and by this means, it distributed the potential cost and risks. As it can be clearly understood from this fact and uttered by the neorealist approach, states – particularly great powers – take into consideration the international organizations and agreements only if there is any gain for them or a function to reduce potential costs of an intervention, which means they make use such organizations as per their interests.

Secondly, excessive armament and military concentration drive expansionist policies to ensure more gaining. Super powers, on the other hand, follow up a strategy to prevent the emergence of a regional hegemonic power. As a matter of fact, in the case study presented above, the attempt of Iraq to become a hegemonic power by means of military concentration was obstructed under the leadership of a super power in the international system. And when diplomatic initiatives to reduce the cost failed, a war was waged in order to ensure the continuity of the system.

Finally, the determinative force of the system was proven although economic reasons and discourse tools were used by Iraq for establishing its hegemony and as a result, Iraq was stopped. The function of the international system is so dominant that India, for instance, supported the coalition forces under the US leadership regardless of its close relations with Iraq.

In conclusion, the arguments of the neorealist approach are well explaining this case study starting with the invasion of Kuwait by Iraq and resulting in the US's intervention by the means of using systematic instruments.

References

Brands, Hal: "Saddam and Israel: What Do the New Iraqi Records Reveal?" *Diplomacy & Statecraft* (22), 2011, pp. 500–520.

Brenner, Michael: "The Alliance: A Gulf Post-Mortem", *International Affairs* 67 (4), 1991, pp. 665–678.

Brown, Eugene: "Contending Paradigms of Japan's International Role: Elite Views of the Persian Gulf Crisis", *Journal of Northeast Asian Studies* 10 (1), 1991, pp. 3–18.

CBC/Radio-Canada: *The Invasion and Annexation of Kuwait*, retrieved 02.08.2019, http://www.cbc.ca/player/Digital+Archives/War+and+Conflict/1991+Gulf+War/ID/1 786746188/?page=3

Cooper, Andrew Fenton, Richard A. Higgott ve Kim Richard Nossal: "Bound to Follow? Leadership and Fellowship in the Gulf Conflict", *Political Science Quarterly* 106 (3), 1991, pp. 391–410.

Cordesman, Anthony H: *Iraq's Military Capabilities: Fighting a Wounded, but Dangerous, Poisonous Snake*, retrieved 03.12.1991 from, http://www.iraqwatch.org/perspectives/csis-iraq_milcap-120301.pdf.

Faırhall, David, Larry Ellıot ve Martin Walker: *Allied Planes Bomb Iraq: Kuwait's Liberation Begun, Says US*, retrieved 17.06.1991 from, www.theguardian.com.

Hartung, William D.: "Breaking the Arms-Sales Addiction: New Directions for U.S. Policy", *World Policy Journal* 8 (1), 1990, pp. 1–26.

Head, William P.: "The Battle for Ra's Al-Khafji and the Effects of Air Power January 29- February 1, 1991", *Air Power History* 60 (2), 2013, pp. 4–15.

Hunter, Shireen: "Persian Gulf Strategy: Beyond the Current Crisis", *International Review* 1990, pp. 20–24.

Huth, William E.: "The Iraq Claims Tribunal: An Overview of the U.N. Compensation Commission", *Dispute Resolution Journal* 54 (2), 1999, pp. 24–83.

Korany, Bahgat: "Oil Power and Arab Politics in the Gulf Crisis", *International Review* 1990, pp. 16–19.

Lawson, Fred H.: "Rethinking the Iraqi Invasion of Kuvait", *The Review of International Affairs* 1 (1), 2001, pp. 1–20.

Maat, Eelco van der: "Sleeping Hegemons: Third-Party Intervention Following Territorial Integrity Transgressions", *Journal of Peace Research* 48 (2), 2011, pp. 201–215.

Malık, J. Mohan: "India's Response to the Gulf Crisis: Implications for Indian Foreign Policy", *Asian Survey* 31 (9), 1991, pp. 847–861.

Mearsheımer, John J.: "Structural Realism", In: Dunne, Tim, Milja Kurki and Steve Smith, (Eds), *International Relations Theories: Discipline and Diversity*, UK: Oxford University Press, 2013, pp. 77–93.

Overseas Development Institute: *The Impact of the Gulf Crisis on Developing Countries*, retrieved 03.03.1991 from, http://www.odi.Org/sites/odi.org.uk/files/odi-assets/publications-opinion-files/ 6770.pdf,

Purrıngton, Courtney and A. K.: "Tokyo's Policy Responses During the Gulf Crisis", *Asian Survey* 31 (4), 1991, pp. 307–323.

Rhodes, Matthew: "Central Europe and Iraq: Balance, Bandwagon, or Bridge?", *Foreign Policy Research Institute* 48 (3), 2004, pp. 423–436.

Sayıgh, Yezid: "The Gulf Crisis: Why the Arab Regional Order Failed", *International Affairs* 67 (3), 1991, pp. 487–507.

Sözen, Ahmet: "A Theoretical Evaluation of Different Faces of Power: US-Turkey Relations Towards Iraq", *Uluslararası İlişkiler* 6 (4), 2010, pp. 55–78.

Sprıngborg, Robert: "Origins of the Gulf Crisis", *Australian Journal of International Affairs* 44 (3), 1990, pp. 221–235.

Steın, Janice Gross: "Deterrence and Compellence in the Gulf, 1990–91: A Failed or Impossible Task?", *International Security* 17 (2), 1992, pp. 147–179.

Steın, Kenneth W.: "Western Intrusion Collides with Tradition in the Middle East", *International Review* 1990, pp. 8–60.

Tétreault, Mary Ann: "Autonomy, Necessity, and the Small State: Ruling Kuwait in the Twentieth Century", *International Organisation* 45 (4), 1991, pp. 565–591.

Tétreault, Mary Ann: "Kuwait's Unhappy Anniversary", *Middle East Policy* 7 (3), 2000, pp. 67–77.

U.S. Messages on July 1990 Meeting of Hussein and American Ambassador, retrieved 13.07.1991 from, http://www.nytimes.com/1991/07/13/world/us-messages-on-july-1990-meeting-of-hussein-and-american-ambassador.html

Walker Martin: "The U.S. and the Persian Gulf Crisis", *World Policy Journal* 7 (4), 1990, pp. 791–799.

Weısburd, A. Mark: "The War in Iraq and the Dilemma of Controlling the International Use of Force", *Texas International Law Journal* (39), 2004, pp. 521–560.

Zenchev, Vladimir, "The Soviet Union and the Gulf Crisis", *International Review*, 17 Ekim 1990, p. 25.

Fatma ÖKDE

III Effects of Economic Crises on Urban Quality of Life

Abstract: The standard of living in urban life is one of the important indicators of the development of a city in today's modern world. The way how the decisions taken are reflected on the individuals and the reactions of the individuals to these decisions affect the decision makers. Especially after the Industrial Revolution, the cities, which had intense migrations, faced unplanned urbanization. Housing and housing problems are some of the burning issues that have been waiting to be solved for many years. In addition to these, infrastructure services and transportation needs were also among the priority issues of big cities. In modern cities these services are now standardized. The living standards and expectations of the urbanite have increased. The urbanite now demands more than the services that meet the basic needs. They have expectations such as social areas, libraries, large green areas and parks, and lively and comfortable trade areas. These expectations are not stable. Along with the changing and developing world, they are in a constant renewal. Local and national governments are facing ever-changing demands. To meet these demands a high budget amount and efficiently planned budget are needed. The economic crises that emerged periodically lead to disruption of these services. This situation also negatively affects the standard of living in urban life.

Keywords: Urban Quality of Life, Economic Crisis, Welfare, Urban Life

Introduction

Urban quality of life is affected by many factors. These factors are divided into objective and subjective factors. Especially as the subjective factors are based on the perception of the urbanite, the effect of the urban services are important. Because individuals today have different expectations. Objective indicators have an important place in the standard of life in urban life of the individual. However, it may be a mistake not to give the necessary importance to the subjective criteria. In today's world, the expectations of the urbanite are changing very quickly. Objective services such as infrastructure services, transportation services, or access to urban facilities are not considered sufficient to improve the standard of living in urban life. Urban services should be provided with an understanding that places the individual in the center. Many services by local governments have become common nowadays. Often urbanites do not consider them to be factors that increase the urban quality of life. For example, routine works such as the collection of waste in time, clean streets, and continuous water supply at all hours of the day and night are not of great importance for the urbanite.

The modern urbanite demands more social facilities, large gardens and parks, a market boom, and a lucrative trade. Local authorities are aware of these demands. For example, they strive to create spaces where a family can spend time with their children, shop, relax, and eat. This situation requires a great economic power. Especially in developing countries, such local services can be put into the second plan considering that resources are limited. Services that can be considered ordinary in developed countries are considered unnecessary in these countries. The fulfillment of basic services for local governments becomes a priority. Disruptions can be seen even in basic services such as providing transportation and infrastructure and collecting waste.

An economic crisis at a global or national level may disrupt local services. The slowdown of the economy has negative effects on individuals as well as on local services. The cuts in local government budgets cause disruptions in urban services. Individuals are negatively affected by economic conditions. Those who lose their jobs or those who suffer from payroll deductions lose their familiar living standards. This situation affects the urban quality of life negatively.

The Urban Quality of Life

The cities reached their present form as a result of the developing urbanization with the industrialization in the nineteenth century. The city, which had been formed as a result of the developments, continued to exist within the framework of various economic, social, political, and physical developments. Cities have renewed themselves from the moment they emerged and adapted to the developments.

The effect of the term "urban quality of life" by gaining importance in many areas has led the term to expand and differ in content of the concept. The multidimensional characteristics of the concept has taken place among the different sciences, social sciences, sciences, and engineering and health sciences. The definition of this diversity varies according to each science. In this context, while the concept of standard of living has been expressed in various definitions, it was used as a concept of luxury and was seen as an unimportant concept in the past. Nowadays, it has gained a total satisfaction meaning for individuals; this satisfaction is seen as the level of fulfillment of requirements, expectations, and desires as well as numerical standards and quantitative satisfaction (Abbate, Giambalvo, and Milito 2001, p. 277).

The urban quality of life consists of a combination of many factors affecting the individual. These factors include social life and social environment, healthy and high standards, and an active economy. Especially the housing and social and physical environment of the individual play an important role in determining the standard of living in urban life (Shookner 1998, p. 545). In addition, the freedom of individuals, personal health status, and relationships with other individuals in the environment are important factors that affect the urban quality of life (WHOQOL, 1995). The standard of living of all people in urban communities is directly related to each other in both natural and man-made environments (Perloff 1969, p. 3).

The indicators of the concept and measurement of urban quality of life are tried to be determined. These indicators seem to be two-dimensional. In the first dimension, it is seen that the concept of urban quality of life contains objective variables related to the life of the individual. In the latter, the standard of living includes subjective variables that are shaped by the perception of these objective variables in the environment (Marans 2007, p. 28). In this context, how the objective and subjective variables that shape the standard of living indicators are determined is the subject. Common variables are present in these variables in which the individuals are highly determinative, and especially subjective variables are composed of quite different indicators because they are shaped according to perception. Many different factors are effective in determining the indicators formed by these variables. Basically, environmental and psychological elements appear to be prominent (Wish 1986, p. 94). The indicators determined for the standard of living are used to determine the indicators of the standard of living in urban life at the point of direct interaction of the individuals with their surroundings in their daily lives, and also the elements peculiar to the city are also addressed.

The Economy and the Urban Quality of Life

The starting point of an individual-centered and consumption-oriented approach to urban quality of life is Maslow's Theory of Hierarchy of Needs. With this theory, an alternative point of view emerged to the concept of urban quality of life both in its definition and its indicators. In his theory, Maslow divided the needs of people to fulfill their functions so that they basically could continue their lives by searching why people have been featuring different needs at different times. This is ranked from 1 to 5, each with separate requirements. In the first stage, physiological requirements such as air, water, food, shelter, etc. and life-sustaining needs are taking place. In the second stage, there are security and safety requirements. As a reflection of being a social being, there are the needs such as love, loyalty, and belonging in the third stage. In the fourth stage there are the needs such as respectability, trust, success, which can be considered as ego needs. The fifth stage is defined as self-realization (Maslow 1970, p. 35–46).

Therefore, each development leads to more expectations for individuals. The fulfillment of basic urban services becomes insufficient for the individual after a while. In order to meet the increasing demands of the urbanite, a strong economy and an active trade area is required.

In order to determine social changes and social trends in societies, since the beginning of the twentieth century states, local governments and some non-governmental organizations have been involved in various studies and statistical studies. As a result of these studies, the research studies of objective and subjective indicators gained momentum. In this context, indicators such as income, education and health expenditures, consumption expenditures, housing status and needs were brought together and a pool of data has been started to be created (Bognar 2005, p. 561).

Economic dynamism and growth are important for cities. Cities are an economic organization, a scene in which social actions are displayed, a corporate process and a symbol of collective union. It is stated that in cities the relations between the primary groups and the institutions with various functions are gathered together. In these relations, the first one refers to the family and neighborhood ties, and the second to the characteristics of the city life (Mumford 2000, p. 93–94). In addition, cities are important in terms of providing freedoms. When we look at the developed urban economies, it is seen that there is an improved freedom structure (Pirenne 2013, p. 57).

Tab. 1 shows the importance of economic conditions in terms of urban quality of life. The income and consumption levels of individuals, real estate market, employment opportunities, and economic viability are indicated as indicators of the economic situation. In addition, when we evaluate the other components of urban quality of life, we see that a strong economy is necessary. For example, a strong economy is required for good health care or for a quality education process.

In the researches on the definition and determining the indicators of the concept of the urban quality of life, the concepts of life satisfaction and happiness stand out generally (McCall 1975, p. 232). This shows the relationship between a strong economy and standard of living in urban life.

The reasons for the changes and transformation of cities include the way the capitalist perspective and the way of life affect the life and social life from their point of view, and the production of the space according to their own

Tab. 1: Urban Quality of Life. **Source** Santos, L. D. and Martins, I. 2007, p. 415.

Environmental Factors	**Common Uses**
Green Fields	Social Facilities
Air Quality	Education and Health Facilities
Water Quality	Urban Heritage
Infrastructure Quality	Ease of Transportation
Economic conditions	**Social Factors**
Income and Consumption	Population
Housing Market	Education and Health
Employment Opportunities	Security
Economic Vitality	Civic Participation

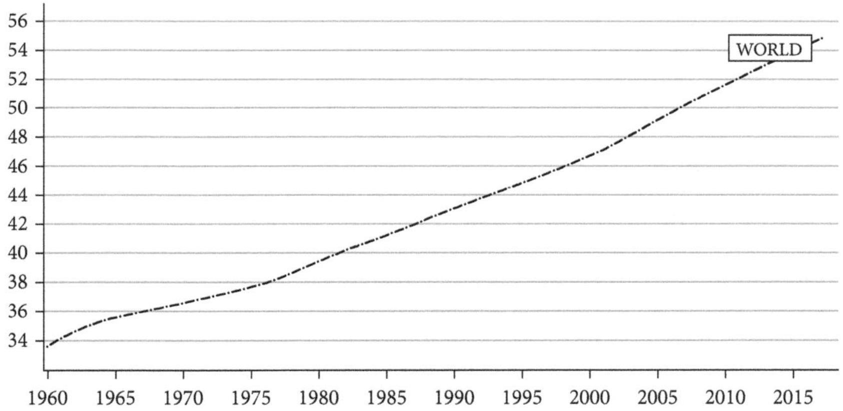

Fig. 1: Urban Population of Total (%, All Countries). Source https://data.worldbank.org/indicator/sp.urb.totl.in.zs

understanding. Therefore, in the societies where capitalism is dominant, the process of urbanization and the development of capital are connected (Harvey 2016, p. 77).

As cities have a strong economy, they increase the standard of living. Cities are a formation that contains many structures and contradictions. The cities, where individuals can reflect themselves, should aim to increase the standard of living by enabling economic gains and a safe life (Harvey 2003, p. 180).

Fig. 1 shows that the urban population is constantly increasing over time. Fig. 2 shows that economic growth rates are horizontally and there are periodic

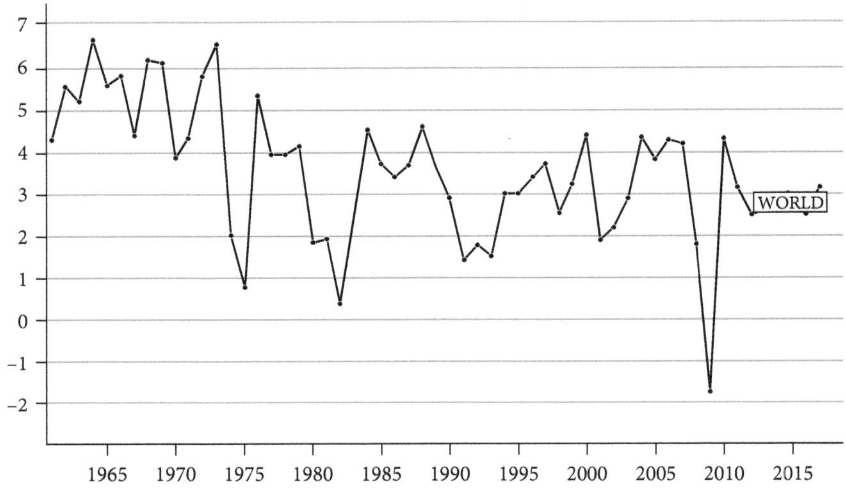

Fig. 2: Economic Growth (%, All Countries). Source https://data.worldbank.org/indicator/ny.gdp.mktp.kd.zg

crises. Cities are the center of economic growth. Most of the economic activities take place in cities. Therefore, the economic crisis in the economy and urban quality of life negatively affect the major crises.

As the world population continues to grow, the population density in cities is rising much faster than in rural areas. This fact, known as urbanization, affects many areas such as agriculture, environment, politics, and energy use. In this case, the discussion of the city administration means the discussion of the future of standard of living we have. If cities are equipped with the right leaders, strategies and financing, urbanization can bring about positive changes in the lives of all of us. Cities are important actors of economic growth and cultural development and can provide us with numerous advantages. Poor management of the rapid growth of urban growth has the potential to disrupt the standard of living as well. It is necessary for the cities that cannot get used to such rapid growth to develop the resources, infrastructure, and leaders and to keep up with the era in line with new strategies.

The cost of crowding caused by the dense population in the cities has become non-negligible. For example, the problem of traffic congestion due to work and travel both reduces the quality of the service and causes a big time and loss of fuel. This dense population, therefore, causes various problems such as housing problems, land problems, squatting problems, infrastructure problems, health, and education problems. The solution of the multifaceted problems caused by the resulting this misery leads to the emergence of a political problem in the national plan as well as technical, administrative, and financial problems. Politicians encourage squatting by making short-term promises to increase their votes. Therefore, along with the preventive measures of over-growth, it is necessary to take measures to mitigate the burden of large cities.

Functional cities and a functioning economy are based on the timely and effective movement of people, information, and goods. The economic prosperity of a region is directly proportional to this movement matrix. Especially in the new age of an idea-based economy, the quality and the number of connections created by people for people and for information are important factor for efficiency. The higher quality a person can achieve on an average day, the more likely it is that the person will add an innovative value to the economy. The ease of dissemination and exchange of ideas is a key factor in an idea-based economy (Burkhalter and Castells 2009, p. 34).

The basic socioeconomic impacts of the crises in the economy on societies are in the form of decreasing income, unemployment and consequently changing life standards negatively, increasing income inequality, and poverty among the social classes. While the World Bank identifies poverty in terms of the lack/absence of monetary income, the United Nations Development Program (UNDP) deals with the concept more broadly. By defining it as being deprived from the opportunities for human development (lifelong health, a creative life, an average standard of living, freedom, self-confidence, dignity, etc.).

People living in low- and middle-income households, particularly in urban areas, reported that the gap was more difficult to close in the crisis by closing the existing gap compared to households with similar income in rural areas. Neighborhood problems in urban areas are more common. In villages or towns, people with the highest income levels report fewer neighborhood problems than those in the three lower quarters (Eurofound, 2014).

Some explanations of why unemployment is so damaging to life satisfaction have emphasized the effects on financial deprivation, while others have emphasized how they break social networks and create social isolation. Evidence from the European Social Survey shows that, although both factors are important, above all, the most important thing that affects life satisfaction is financial deprivation. For the person who suffered from unemployment, it has effect more than half of his wife's influence (Gallie, 2013).

However, reactions to global crises should also play a strong role for cities. So far, cities are perceived as the "engines" of national economies and there is no reason to drop this idea. As a matter of fact, the city authorities find themselves at least in a position to increase the production in the real sector of the economy by increasing employment and income generation at the local level. Efficient, multi-faceted institutional, policy, and budgetary ties between all governmental stakeholders are necessary if urban responses to economic crises need to be influential on a local scale, which has positive regional or national repercussions (multiplier effects). In this context, proper alignment of central and local government spending at the city level may facilitate transfers and effective use by city authorities (Unhabitat, 2013).

The emphasis of locality evolved into nationalism after the Middle Age. However, as a result of the economic crises in the development stages of capitalism, locality has come to the fore again with the discourse and practice of globalization. The 1970s witnessed another crises of the capitalism and since the 1980s neo-liberal policies have been exported from Britain and the United States to other parts of the world to overcome this crisis. Today, the position of the local in the global one is changing the conception of the nation and the national that the classical economy based on, and the neoclassical economy emphasizes the importance of the local and parallel cities in the process of globalization. Parallel to the weakening of the concept of nationality along with the effects of globalization, the cities re-emerged as actors on the stage of history.

The problem of poverty, which is an important obstacle for people to live a balanced and peaceful life by participating in social life, continues to exist in all over the world. The state, which has been trying to take the necessary measures to minimize this problem by fulfilling the necessity of being a social state, has been obliged to make concessions from the social policies it has implemented from time to time due to the economic crises. The effects of these economic crises can be seen on the attitude of the state toward the need for housing, which is one of the most basic human needs from time to time.

Conclusion

Urban life quality is an important variable in today's modern life. Changing living standards and expectations change standards regarding quality of life. Therefore, determining the quality of urban life is not easy. There are objective and subjective criteria in determining the quality of urban life. Economics has an important place in both of these criteria. Especially the thoughts of individuals about their income and wealth is very important. Does an individual who is able to meet his basic needs live in prosperity? Does the improvement in objective indicators positively affect subjective indicators? It is not easy to answer these questions. But the fact is that the economy is extremely effective in determining the quality of urban life.

For many years, cities have been the basis of the economy and therefore the population is constantly increasing in the cities. In order for every individual to benefit from economic growth, the economy must grow continuously. However, the capitalist economic system operates differently. There is a cyclical process with periodic ups and downs. National and global economic crises are part of the current economic system. Global economic growth rates in the history of modern economies have experienced sharp declines. The effect of this situation on individuals can be very tragic.

In economic growth periods, individuals form a standard of living. It is thought that the welfare achieved in these periods will be permanent. This is understandable because of the human nature. However, along with the economic crises, this thought may be damaged. The urban quality of life is affected negatively by crises. This effect occurs in two ways. First, the decline in the income level of the individual negatively affects the quality of urban life. Secondly, reductions in central government and local government spending are seen. Deficiencies in public services also negatively affect the quality of urban life.

References

Abbate, Riccardo, Giambalvo, Ornella, and Milito, Anna Maria: "Service and Life Quality: The Case of Palermo", *Social Indicators Research* (54), 2001, pp. 275–308.

Bognar, Greg: "The Concept of Quality of Life", *Social Theory Practise* 31(4), 2005, pp. 561–580.

Burkhalter, Laura, and Castells, Manuel: "Beyond the Crisis: Towards a New Urban Paradigm", In: Qu, L., Yang, C., Hui, X., Sepúlveda, D. (Eds.), *The New Urban Question: Urbanism Beyond Neo-Liberalism*, 4th Conference of International Forum on Urbanism. International Forum on Urbanism, 2009, pp. 21–44.

Eurofound: *Quality of Life in Urban and Rural Europe*. Luxembourg: Publications Office of the European Union, 2014.

Gallie, Duncan: *Economic Crisis, Quality of Work and Social Integration: Topline Results from Rounds 2 and 5 of the European Social Survey*. London: Centre for Comparative Social Surveys, 2013.

Harvey, Duncan: "Debates and Developments the Right to the City". *International Journal of Urban and Regional Research* 27(4), 2003, pp. 939–941.

Harvey, Duncan: *Sosyal Adalet ve Şehir*. Çev. Mehmet Moralı, İstanbul: Metis Yayıncılık, 2016.

Marans. Robert: "Kentsel Yaşam Kalitesinin Ölçülmesi". *Mimarlık Dergisi* (335), 2007, pp. 1–5.

Maslow, Abraham: *Motivation and Personality*. New York: Harper & Row Publishers. 1970.

McCall, Storrs.: "Quality of life". *Social Indicators Research* (2), 1975, pp. 229–248.

Mumford, Lewis: "What Is a City?" In R. T. LeGates & F. Stout (Ed.). *The City Reader*. New York: Routledge, 2000.

Perloff, Harvey (Ed.): "The Quality of the Urban Environment", *Resource for the Future*. Washington D.C., 1969

Pirenne, Henry: *Ortaçağ Kentleri*. Çev. Şadan Karadeniz, İstanbul: Iletişim Yayınları, 2012.

Santos, Luis Delfim and Martins, Isabel: "Monitoring Urban Quality of Life: The Porto Experience". *Social Indicators Research* (80), 2007, pp. 411–425.

Shookner Malcolm: "A Quality of Life Index for Ontario". *CSLS Conference on the State of Living Standards and the Quality of Life in Canada*, Ontario Social Development Council, 1998.

Unhabitat: *State of the World's Cities 2012/2013 Prosperity of Cities*. London: Routledge, 2013.

Wish, Naomi Bailin: "Are We Really Measuring the Quality of Life? Well Being Has Subjective Dimensions, As Well As Objective Ones". *American Journal of Economics and Sociology* 45 (1), 1986, p. 94.

World Health Organization: "The WHO Quality of Life Assessment Instrument". *Quality of Life Research* (10), 1995, pp. 711–721.

WorldBank: *GDP growth (annual %)*, retrieved 03.05.2019 from, https://data.worldbank.org/indicator/ny.gdp.mktp.kd.zg.

WorldBank: *Urban population (% of total)*, retrieved 03.05.2019 from, https://data.worldbank.org/indicator/sp.urb.totl.in.zs.

Assist Prof. Dr. Habib DEMİRHAN

IV European Union Debt Crisis: Debt Consolidation and Measures for the Crisis

Abstract: In 2008, the world economy faced with a global financial crisis. The crisis affected the world economy deeply so that its effects are compared with Great Depression. In 2010, Eurozone faced with debt crisis. This crisis began in Ireland and then spread to Portugal and Greece. The debt crisis was the first crisis in the Euro zone, which was founded in 1999. In the historical process we witness that crises occur due to different reasons. In every period, measures and precautions taken against crises vary.In this study, after briefly reviewing the process leading to the historical process of the EU and monetary union, the reasons of debt crisis will be examined and the measures taken by the countries and the Union will be briefly evaluated.

Keywords: Crisis, Debt Crisis, Eurozone, Fiscal Consolidation

Introduction

The twentieth century was the years of integrations worldwide. These integrations have been established for different reasons such as political, economic, cultural, geographic, etc. However, the basis of all integrations has always been the economic concerns. The reasons underlying economic integration are: to be able to withstand the competitive conditions and to increase their productivity. The countries that come together with these aims are trying to liberalize themselves within the framework of different economic and cooperation agreements. The process leading to the European Union has been shaped within this framework. The first economic integration was established between Belgium, Netherlands and Luxembourg. For this reason, the integration is named Benelux. The aim of the integration was theoretically to create a custom union between these countries. On May 1950, Robert Schuman, French Minister of Exterior, was proposed to combine the coal-steel resources between France and Germany and the production and use of these substances, which are the basic inputs of the war industry should be under the responsibility of an international institution. These proposal is mostly known as the Schuman Declaration. On June 1950 with the participation of Belgium, France, Germany, Italy, Luxembourg and the Netherlands, negotiations that aimed at creating a common market for iron and steel market began. On April 18, 1951, the Paris Treaty establishing the European Coal Steel Community was signed in Paris. This agreement, valid for 50 years, ended on

July 23, 2002. On September 25, 1952, the European Coal Steel Community was established. The success of the European Coal Steel Community has led to a growing emphasis on the realization of a wider economic union in Europe that is not sector-based. In 1957, Rome Treaty was signed to establish two new institutions. These institutions were European Economic Community (EEC) and European Atomic Energy Community (EURATOM).

The agreements that established European Coal and Steel Community, European Economic Community and European Atomic Energy Community have been the basis for the establishment of European Union. Nowadays, the European Union (EU) is claimed as the largest political and economic integration.

In 2010, Eurozone faced with debt crisis. The future of EU has been questioned after this crisis within the context of Maastricht criteria. The study aims to explain the measures taken by both member states and the union to overcome the results of the crisis.

The Brief History of European Union

There are 28 member countries of EU. Since 1950s, EU completes the stage of economic integration, such as customs union, single market, economic union and monetary union, while on one hand has been expanding geographically and politically with the participation of new countries and on the other hand developing towards, its long term goal, political unity. In this long process, undoubtedly, very important steps have been taken so far such as the removal of barriers to trade in goods and services between member states, establishing single foreign trade policies against non-member countries, ensuring the free movement of production factors among member countries, harmonization of national economic policies, the creation of a monetary union called Eurozone, and more importantly, monopolizing of monetary policies among member countries.

Major decisions were taken in the field of Eurozone and member criteria for EU in 1990s. In 1993, the criteria of being a member which is also called Copenhagen Criteria, were defined in Copenhagen Summit. The Maastricht Treaty, signed in 1992 and entered into force in 1993, defined the Eurozone criteria. In other words, with this treaty, Convergence criteria that EU member states must fulfil to enter Eurozone were defined. These convergence criteria are:

- *Price Stability*: It is measured by inflation rate (costumer price). It should not be more than 1.5 percentage points above the rate of the three best performing Member States.

- *Sound Public Finance*: It is measured by government deficit as % of GDP. It should not be more than 3 %. It is accepted as reference value.
- *Sustainable Public Finance*: It is measured by government debt as % of GDP. It should not be more than 60 %.
- *Durability of Convergence*: It is measured by long-term interest rates. It should not be more than 2 percentage points above the rate of three best performing Member States in terms of price stability.
- *Exchange Rate Stability*: It is measured by deviation from a central rate. The convergence criterion is defined as participation in the EU's Exchange Rate Mechanism II for at least 2 years without severe tensions. Participation in this mechanism is voluntary.

In the early 2000s, the Constitutional Treaty debates began. With the Constitutional Treaty, which was planned to replace other previously signed treaties, it was aimed to close the democratic deficit and to activate the decision-making mechanism. The Treaty would also refer to EU symbols that could be linked to the political union, even indirectly, such as the EU flag and the EU anthem (Arisan 2010, p. 3). This agreement was rejected by the 2005 referendum by the founding members of EU, France and Netherlands, and this was the beginning of one of the major crises in EU history. The content of the treaty was changed. Even the Constitutional Treaty name was set aside and the name of the treaty was changed to the Reform Treaty. Reform Treaty was named Lisbon Treaty just after it was signed by EU leaders in Lisbon in 2007.

The Treaty of Lisbon, which entered into force on December 1, 2009, has set the framework for a stronger European democracy, a more effective and transparent decision-making mechanism and the increasing participation of European citizens, and has also provided a potential to gain political power in the international platform that will balance its economic weight.

EU Debt Crisis (Eurozone Crisis)

During the global financial crisis, the European Union was going through a very difficult period. The process, which started with the failure of the Constitutional Treaty, discussed since 2000s and the substitution of the Lisbon Treaty as the Reform Treaty, in 2008, the year of the global economic crisis, caught EU with ratification process of the Lisbon Treaty. The EU countries, which were caught unprepared for the crisis, did not perform very successfully in the fight against the effects of the crisis due to the lack of definitive provisions on the coordination of economic and fiscal policies in the EU treaties. There were serious problems in countries with a high share of financial services in GDP such as the UK, Ireland and Spain. The global crisis effected the new EU member states more than others. For example, in Latvia, national income decreased by 20 % in 2009. In addition to Latvia, Hungary and Romania were forced to apply to the International Monetary Fund.

However, the coordination of the responsible behavior (also referred as "coordination reflex" of years of working together) of some EU member states leaders in this area prevented the crisis from being catastrophic but it could not prevent the low growth rates and high unemployment (Tsoulakis et al. 2009). Following the entry into force of the Treaty of Lisbon, a multi-dimensional economic/financial crisis took place in Greece. This crisis was important with its reasons and consequences in determining the future of EU. The new government, which came to a head in the autumn of 2009, shocked EU officials and markets by announcing that the ratio of the budget deficit to national income reached 12.7 % – nearly twice the rate announced by the previous government. Most importantly, the total public debt in Greece was around 125 % of the country's national income. In addition, Eurozone credibility has been significantly shaken and the euro lost value against the dollar while it was coming out that Greece falsified its macroeconomic indicator (Maastricht criteria indicators) to be a member of Eurozone. However, the situation that led to the questioning of Eurozone was not merely lack of audit; another, and perhaps even the most important, problem was the inability of the legal and institutional infrastructure to provide the necessary coordination in economic/fiscal policies in a structure in which the sovereignty of monetary policy and exchange rate policy was completely transferred to the European Central Bank, in accordance with the Economic and Monetary Union requirements.

In fact, although the monetary policy of the EPB was solid, the fact that the lack of coordination in economic/fiscal policies would lead to serious problems in the future was the subject of several debates at the end of the 1990s, when the Economic and Monetary Union was established.

Fiscal Consolidation

The classical finance theory defines borrowing as a method of financing that should be applied when normal public revenues, such as financing large public works services, are inadequate to meet public services and in extraordinary situations and conditions such as war. They argued that, in normal circumstances, public services should be financed by taxes. As a result of the changes and preferences in technological, social, political and economic conditions in today's world, borrowing within the modern financial approach has become a normal public income. Although various limitations are tried to be made, borrowing, in the financing of public investments and expenditures, is a frequently used financing method. Borrowing is considered as the collection of future tax revenues from this day. For this reason, governments can easily use the borrowing due to the resistance of taxpayers to tax increases.

Consolidation as a term is defined "the process of being uniting: the quality or state of being united" by *Webster's Dictionary*. Consolidation is an outstanding debt management process in terms of public borrowing. Debt consolidation means "combining more than one debt obligation into a new loan with a favorable term structure such as lower interest rate structure, tenure etc., in exceptional cases where states do not have the possibility to pay due/upcoming debts. In debt management, first of all, it is noted that whether income and expenses balance each other. The countries that have decided to debt consolidation cannot recycle their debts and even pay the interest of their debts. Countries in this situation have lost their debt management capabilities.

The consolidation, which the state can implement against both its domestic and external debts, can be realized in two ways: mandatory and discretionary. In discretionary consolidation, the creditor is free whether or not to replace the short-term credit instrument with a long-term bond. In mandatory consolidation, no choice is given to the creditor. The state consolidates its short-term debt by replacing it with long-term debt or by declaring that it only extends the terms without making such a change by a unilaterally decision. In doing so, it also makes a unilateral decision to provide some compensatory benefits to the creditors, for example by giving higher interest, to satisfy them or not.

Fıscal Consolidation and Its Instruments

Unlike debt consolidation, fiscal consolidation refers to the economic policies of governments to reduce their budget deficits. Governments undertake fiscal consolidation by using various fiscal policy instruments to reduce public spending and increase public revenues. The first measure to reduce budget deficits is to re-establish the balance of income-expenditure in the budget. For this purpose, various deductions are made on the spending items of the budget such as:

- Cancellation of non-urgent public projects and investments in order to re-establish the balance of income and expenditure under current political and economic conditions

- Reduction of transfer expenditures
- Reduction of the number of personnel working in the public sector
- Changes in retirement age and conditions
- Reduction of defense expenditures
- Abolition of some units

In addition to these measures, providing the primary budget surplus (primary surplus) to reduce the increasing interest burden on the budget in particular is another fiscal consolidation method that governments often use. In the implementation of primary surplus, except interest expenditures, governments tend to reduce the public debts stock by creating a budget surplus. Thus, the interest overburden on the debt stock and on budget is decreasing year by year (Emil et al. 2005).

Recently, fiscal rules proposals as an automatic stabilization policy instrument constitute another policy instrument that comes up in fiscal consolidation practices. Thanks to the financial rules formulated in the form of legal and constitutional rules, it is thought that the budget and debt balances can be established without being affected by the politicians and bureaucrats who are willing to pay rent (Savaş 1993).

One of the financial consolidation methods is the privatization policies that emerged with the neoliberal policies towards reducing the share of the state in the real economy in the 1980s. With the state's privatization policy, on one hand it is aimed to transfer inefficient public investments to the private sector while on the other hand to use revenues of privatizations to finance budget and to reduce debt burden. Another method used to finance budget deficit is the increase of tax revenues. However, these measures do not always provide sufficient effect on their own. Citizens have a high tax resistance. Moreover, the economic and social conditions of the country are effective on tax revenues. Particularly in developing countries, it is necessary to make structural reforms in tax systems, and to reduce tax losses and tax evasions. In countries that do not have comprehensive tax reform, the establishment of a budget balance can be achieved by increasing the share of indirect taxes. Thus, the increase of indirect tax share causes a disruptive impact on income distribution, and in the long term state's social transfer expenditures increase.

The Reasons, Effects and Outcomes of Fiscal Consolidation

Financial consolidation are policies aimed at reducing public expenditures and increasing public revenues. For this reason, they may cause a decline in demand especially in the periods of economic recession and increase unemployment and deepen the economic crisis. A recession and crisis conditions were observed in EU countries in early 2008. In the post-2002 period, the growth rates of EU member states have fallen, and unemployment has become an important and structural problem (Kibritçioğlu 2011).

Measures for Debt Crisis in European Union

During the debt crisis both EU member states and EU have taken various measures to overcome effects of the crisis. In this section, measures taken by member states and by the union will be examined.

Measures of Member States

The fiscal policy of member states has been questioned after the debt crisis. The Union made some recommendations to the member states to take necessary measures in compliance with Maastricht criteria. In this section the measures that have been taken by member states will be examined.

Greece

Greece has started implementing serious austerity policies to reduce the impact of the crisis. In 2010, Greece decided to lower the budget deficit by 3 % per year since 2012. The European Commission supported Greece's plan but called on the Greek government to take additional measures. In this context, on March 5, 2010, a package covering wage cuts and increasing taxes was prepared in the public sector. With the measures in the package, the value-added tax (VAT) rate has been increased from 19 % to 23 % and the premiums in the public sector have been cut by 30 %. In addition to VAT, taxes on fuel, cigarette and alcoholic products were increased, 8 % of salaries of public employees were cut, bonuses given to workers were removed and pension reforms were made. The retirement age for women was increased from 60 to 65. The Greek government has adopted a tax reform law aimed at overcoming the tax-evasion problem and imposing higher taxes on high-income groups. In addition, tax is imposed on church, lands and fields belonging to church that is in a privileged position that is not subject to taxation. The average VAT rate has been raised. The government also increased taxes on certain commodities such as fuel, tobacco and alcohol (Nelson et al. 2011: p. 6).

Spain

Spain was another country that have experienced hard days in terms of both debt stock and budget deficits during the crisis period. The Government of Spain announced that it will implement its austerity program steadfastly. In

2010, it was decided that civil servant salaries would be reduced by 5 percent and frozen in 2011. In addition to the reduction of expenditures and pensions, it was decided to reduce public employment. Finally, within the framework of the consolidation process in the banking sector, four Spanish banks were merged in order to strengthen their solvency and assets. In the last days of May 2011, Spain approved the first cut in the salaries of public employees in order to tighten the belt and said that the GDP will grow by 1.3 percent in 2011 by lowering the economic growth forecast (Marti and Perez 2016). These harsh measures have led to a change in government in Spain after Greece and Italy. In the election held on November 21, the conservative People's Party (PP) came into power.

Portugal

Portugal, one of the weakest countries in the EU debt crisis, together with Spain and Greece, came under pressure to take austerity measures together with Spain after the adoption of the 750 billion-euro rescue package adopted at the summit of EU leaders in May 2010. Portugal's aid package agreement with the International Monetary Fund (IMF), the European Central Bank and the European Commission included a tight program to reduce the fiscal deficit for the period 2011–2013. The 2011–2013 agreement stipulated a cuts in local government as well as for central government, decrease of the number of public employees, freezing of public wages for a period of four years, contraction in health benefits and revision in public-private cooperation.

In line with these objectives, a number of measures were planned to be implemented in order to reduce the wages of the employees to GDP by 10 % by 2013, including an average of 5 % wage cuts in the public sector and the limitation of personnel employment. In addition to these cuts, which include top executives in the public sector, large public works, such as the construction of the new international airport, planned to be built in the capital, Lisbon, and some of the high-speed railway construction projects, have been postponed. Moreover, it is aimed to reduce borrowing costs through privatization. Some regulations in the field of taxation, such as increasing of motorway entry fees, increasing of standard VAT rate from 21 % to 23 %, limitation of individual income tax deductions and other tax benefits and increasing of social security contributions, has been done (Caldas 2012).

Italy

In Italy, the Berlusconi Government committed to aiming to reduce the budget deficit rate from 4.6 % in 2010 to 2.7 % in 2012 and announced a € 2.4 billion recovery package. It was announced that about 47 billion euros of new savings measures will be put into effect. Until 2013, wages in the public sector were frozen. In the 2011 budget, 5.5 billion Euro cuts were planned, while ministerial spending was cut by 10 %. Twenty-seven percent extra budgetary funds were removed. The retirement age was indexed to the average life expectancy.

Despite the decreases observed in the asset quality and profitability of banks in the process of crisis and the increasing credit risks, the main effects of the crisis in the economy of the country, where the banking sector displayed a relatively better outlook, was seen in the real sector. The country experienced the biggest recession since World War II and unemployment increased by 1.9 percent compared to the pre-crisis period. In the crisis period, borrowing and budget deficits increased. While the ratio of public debt to GDP, which was 103.5 percent before the crisis, increased to 115.8 percent in 2009, the ratio of budget deficits to GDP increased from 1.5 percent to 5.3 percent (Falagiardi and Gregori 2015, p. 295).

Measures of European Union for Crisis

The future of the EU has been questioned during the debt crisis. The union started to search new ways to strengthen the unity. For this reason, the Union explored some mechanisms to overcome the results of debt crisis. In this section these mechanisms will be examined.

Balance of Payment Facility

The aim of the balance-of-payments fund, established by the Treaty of Rome, was to provide financial assistance to the member countries outside the Euro Area, in the form of loans, in order to maintain the financial stability and balance of the European Community common market. The financial structure of the fund is created by IMF support and revenues of EU Commission bonds. Bonds issued by the EU Commission are issued with the assurance of purchase by the member countries of the Union. The Council of Ministers decides on the amount of credit to be provided to the countries requesting assistance from the fund and the way in which the loan is provided. The specified conditions are finalized by a memorandum of understanding between the Member State and the EU Commission and submitted to the European Parliament and the Council of Ministers of the EU.

Pooled Loans (Greek Loan Facility)

The Credit Pool was established by the EU with the IMF to provide credit to Greece due to the economic crisis based on the authority of the Union to take

Tab. 1: Provided Amount of Credit to Greece (By July 2011, Billion Euro). Source: Colasanti, 2016.

Date of Payment	Eurozone	IMF	Total
May 2010	14,5	5,5	20
September 2010	6,5	2,5	9
December 2010/January 2011	6,5	2,5	9
March 2011	10,9	4,1	15
June 2011	8,7	3,3	12
December 2011	5,8	2,2	8
Total	52,9	20,1	73

action and the excessive budget deficit procedure, regulated in both article 136 and article 126 of the Treaty on the Functioning of European Union. The European Commission contributed 80 billion euros and the IMF 30 billion euros to the Pooled Loans. As shown in Tab. 1, a total of 65 billion euro loans were extended to Greece from July to July 2011 in total.

It is the first financial support program, for Greece, agreed in May 2010. It consisted of bilateral loans from euro area countries and loan from the IMF.

European Financial Stability Mechanism

European Financial Stability Mechanism (EFSM), which is open to all financially disadvantaged EU member states, was established with the Council Regulation No. 407-/2010 on May 11, 2010, to guarantee the financial stability of the union, which lost its stability with the recent severe economic crises and the future of the Euro. As in other union regulations regulating financial stability, the origin of this mechanism is the official Treaty on European Union (the Maastricht Treaty). According to Article 122 of this treaty, it is regulated to help the members whose financial structure has been damaged by being affected by external shocks such as a natural disaster or crisis. Criticisms were made that Greece has an inadequate public finances, gives unrealistic information to EUROSTAD and does not fully meet the reasons laid down in Article 122.

EFSM is a temporary stabilization mechanism. As of June 2013, the EFSM has been replaced by the European Stability Mechanism (ESM). Ireland and Portugal benefited from EFSM. The mechanism is financed through bonds guaranteed by the EU Budget. The size of the EFSM, where all transactions are carried out in Euro, is EUR 60 billion. The countries benefiting from EFSM credits are obliged to implement the economic stability program to be determined by the

Commission. The use of the loan is also subject to the audit of the European Court of Auditors and European Anti-Fraud Office (OLAF).

European Financial Stability Facility

European Financial Stability Facility (EFSF), established as a limited liability company under the laws of Luxembourg on June 7, 2010, with the participation of Eurozone countries under the decision of the Economic and Financial Affairs Council (ECOFIN) on May 9, 2010, provides temporary financial support to Euro Zone countries with various debt problems in order to maintain monetary union. Like the European Financial Stability Mechanism, EFSF was also temporary and replaced by the European Stability Mechanism after 2013.

European Stability Mechanism

A new stabilization mechanism, covering EFSF and EFSM, has been established with the decision of Council of Europe on December 17, 2010. The paragraph "*The Member States whose currency is the euro may establish a stability mechanism to be activated if indispensable to safeguard the stability of the euro area as a whole. The granting of any required financial assistance under the mechanism will be made subject to strict conditionality*" has been added to Article 136 of the Treaty on the Functioning of the European Union by European Council Decision in order to provide legal basis for ESM (*Official Journal of European Union* 2011, p. 27). ESM will work in close cooperation with the IMF, another financial institution providing financial assistance. The beneficiary country will receive technical and financial assistance and support from the IMF as well as the conditions set by the ESM. The governing bodies of ESM are the Board of Governors and the Board of Directors. The Boards of Governors is chaired by the president of Eurogroup. Each Member contributes to the ESM authorized capital based its respective share of the EU total population and gross domestic product (https://www.esm.europa.eu/esm-governance, 20.04.2019).

Euro-Plus Pact

On February 4, 2011, Germany and France proposed the foundation of a pact in the fields of education, public finance stability and R&D (Research and Development) within the Union. For this reason, Euro-Plus Pact has been founded. One of the most important mechanism to ensure better economic governance after the sovereign debt crisis in the Eurozone is Euro-Plus Pact. At first it had been called the "competitiveness pact". Although this new pact was

Tab. 2: Shares and Capital per ESM Member. **Source:** Retrieved from https://www.esm.europa.eu/esm-governance (Accessed date: 20.04.2019).

ESM Members	ESM key(%)	Number of Shares	Subscribed Capital (€ 000)	Paid-in capital (€ 000)
Austria	2.7632	194,753	19,475,300	2,226,720
Belgium	3.4519	243,285	24,328,500	2,781,680
Cyprus	0.1948	13,733	1,373,300	156,960
Estonia	0.1847	13,020	1,302,000	148,800
Finland	1.7844	125,768	12,576,800	1,437,920
France	20.2381	1,426,383	142,638,300	16,308,720
Germany	26.9496	1,899,406	189,940,600	21,717,120
Greece	2.7962	197,078	19,707,800	2,253,360
Ireland	1.5806	111,404	11,140,400	1,273,760
Italy	17.7839	1,253,406	125,340,600	14,330,960
Latvia	0.2746	19,353	1,935,300	221,200
Lithuania	0.4063	28,634	2,863,400	261,760
Luxemburg	0.2486	17,521	1,752,100	200,320
Malta	0.0726	5,117	511,700	58,480
Netherlands	5.6756	400,015	40,001,500	4,573,600
Portugal	2.4910	175,566	17,556,600	2,007,360
Slovakia	0.8184	57,680	5,768,000	659,200
Slovenia	0.4679	32,977	3,297,700	342,080
Spain	11.8174	832,888	83,288,800	9,522,960
Total	**100.00**	**7,047,987.00**	**704,798,700.00**	**80,482,960.00**

intended to represent a particular commitment by Eurozone member countries, many non-euro Member States have also signed up. The main objectives of Euro-Plus Pact are (Gros and Alcidi 2011, p. 85):

- To increase competitiveness
- To increase employment
- To increase the sustainability of public finances
- To strengthen financial stability

Fiscal Union

Fiscal union as a term tends to have different meanings in the policy literature, with interpretations ranging from a set of common fiscal rules to the creation of a fully federal government with tax and spending authority (Thirion 2017,

p. 3). Dabrowski (2015) defines fiscal Union as "transfers of parts of fiscal resources and competences in the area of fiscal policy and fiscal management from the national to supranational level". The foundation of a fiscal Union was always in the agenda of EU. The Eurozone Crisis brought this idea on agenda again.

In order to overcome the financial crisis in the EU, a proposal for a financial union under the leadership of Germany and France has come to the agenda. Although the UK rejected the proposal for the establishment of a financial union with Hungary at the last EU Summit, 17 countries in the Eurozone and 9 member countries which are not the member of Eurozone reached a preliminary agreement on the progress of fiscal union. The fiscal union proposal included the measurements such as establishment of a common tax regime in the EU countries, in particular the corporate tax, submission of Member State budgets to EU Commission approval, and implementation of fiscal policies that are not approved by the Union is subject to sanctions. In addition to the Maastricht criteria, which constitute the monetary union, the proposal of the financial union is a step toward a more stringent economic cooperation and a step toward completing the missing financial union.

Conclusion

Since 1950s EU aims to complete its social, political and economic integration. In 1990s, the Copenhagen Criteria has been accepted to regulate political dimension while Maastricht criteria has aimed to regulate economic criteria. In 2010 debt crisis, especially Maastricht criteria has been questioned by the Union. In particular, it was come out that despite not meeting Maastricht convergence criteria, Greece was allowed to join the Union for political reasons.

After 2010 Debt crisis, the union made some recommendations to the countries such as Greece, Spain, Italy and Portugal in order to regulate their fiscal policies within the context of Maastricht convergence criteria. The EU also started to discuss some economic mechanism in itself for a strong economic structure.

It has been explored that the meeting of Maastricht convergence criteria is important and vital for the future of the Union. It should not be flexible and vary across countries. If EU aims complete its economic and political integration, the implementation of fiscal rules should be inflexible. An integration of fiscal policy within the Union is not possible and countries will not transfer their authorities to the union in this field. For this reason, the Union at least should control the budgetary process and other instruments rigidly.

References

Arısan, Eralp Nilgün: "Avrupa Birliğinde Neler Oluyor", *TEPAV Değerlendirme Notları* 2010, pp. 1–7.

Caldas, Jose Castro: *The Impact of "Anti-Crisis" Measures and the Social and Employment Situation*, retrieved 21.04.2019 from http://www. eesc. europa. eu/resources/docs/portugal-en.

Colasanti, Fabio: "Financial Assistance to Greece: Three Programmes". *European Policy Center Discussion Paper* (6345), February 2016, pp. 1–100.

Council of the European Communities: *Treaty on European Union (The Maastricht Treaty)*. Brussels.

Council of the European Union: *The Lisbon Treaty*. Brussels, 2007.

Dabrowski, Marek: "Monetary Union and Fiscal and Macroeconomic Governance", *European Economy Paper, European Commission, Fellowship initiative 2014–2015, Discussion paper* (13), 2015, pp. 1–44.

Emil, Ferhat, Yılmaz Hakan H. and Rijckeghem Caroline: *Kamu Borcu Nasıl Oluştu*. İstanbul: TESEV, 2005.

Falagiardi, Matteo and Gregori, Wildmer Daniel: "The Impact of Fiscal Policy Announcements by the Italian Government on the Sovereign Spread: A Comparative Analysis". *European Journal of Political Economy* (39), 2015, pp. 288–304.

Gros, Daniel and Alcidi, Cinzia: "Sense and Nonsense of the Euro-Plus Pact". *The 2011 TGAE Report* 2011, pp.83–90.

Marti, Francisco and Perez, Javier J: "Spanish Public Finances through the Financial Crisis". *Documentos de Trabajo* (1620), 2016, pp. 1–35.

Nelson, M. Rebecca, Belkin, Paul and Mix, E. Derek: "Greece's Debt Crisis: Overview, Policy Responses, and Implications", *Congressional Research Service* 7–5700, 2011, pp. 1–24.

Official Journal of European Union: Decisions: *European Council Decision, L91/1*, retrieved 21.04.2019 from, https://eur-lex.europa.eu/LexUriServ/LexUriServ.do?uri=OJ:L:2011:091:0001:0002:. EN:PDF

Thirion, Gilles: "European Fiscal Union: Economic Rationale and Design Challenges". *CEPS Working Document* (1), 2017, pp. 1–38.

Tsoulakis, Loukas, Cramme, Olaf. and Liddle, Roger: *An EU "Fit for Purpose" in the Global Age: Can We Rise to the Challenge?*, retrieved 15.05.2019 from, www.policy-network.net.

Asst. Prof. Dr. Burak ÖKDE

V The Role of the Economic Crisis to Expand the Public Sector

Abstract: The small size of the public sector has long been seen as the key to economic growth. However, it is seen that public expenditures have an increasing tendency. As one of the reasons for this situation, we can show liberal economy. The liberal economy, which is ironically trying to keep state intervention to a minimum, can also be the cause of this situation. High-risk capital causes crises from time to time. In such cases, the public sector is seen as a savior. And the public sector loves to intervene in the economy and uses every opportunity to grow. So, this study aims to demonstrate the impact of economic crises in the rise of public spending and criticizing the savior role of the public sector. Public spending in times of crisis can have positive effects in the short term. But in the long term, the effects of the large public sector on the economy should be discussed. Because, if public spending increases once, it is very difficult to draw it back to its former level.

Keywords: Public Spending, Economic Crisis, Private Sector

Introduction

Public spending was discussed before in the modern states as it is now. The reason for this discussion is the realization of public expenditures by taxes. Taxes transfer the wealth of individuals or institutions to the state. Can this wealth be used efficiently by the state? For many years and experiences, the answer to this question is no. When democracy is not fully settled, it is understandable that no account is asked about how taxes are spent. For this reason, the first efforts were seen in industrialization.

The industrial revolution has initiated one of the most destructive wars. From the 1850s, the industrial revolution began to destroy the old world and began to create a new one (Dowd 2004, p. 45). In this process, the meanings attributed to the public sector have changed.

State structures and features were re-established. In addition, the private sector and the companies also were developed, and the revenues and the capitals they controlled increased. Thus, the ideas of liberal economists against state intervention have begun to strengthen.

Criticisms Towards the Public Sector

According to Adam Smith, the State's areas of duty are limited. However, even if the state remains within these limits, it may cause corruption and inefficiency. A person applying for a trial comes with a bribe to seek rights, in this case he can get more than his right. The person who comes with a smaller bribe may be the wronged party. In addition, cases of delaying the decision to continue bribery can also be seen (Smith 1776, p. 796).

Adam Smith has included infrastructure services among state duties. These services, which make trade easier for citizens are seen among the necessary jobs (Smith 1776, p. 805). Another duty of the State is to take the necessary security measures to ensure the healthy and proper trade. While taking these measures, certain amounts of taxes on the trade made are seen plausible (Smith 1776, p. 816).

Ricardo states that the biggest obstacle to production is taxes to finance public spending. The taxes collected reduce the capital to be used. Taxes have negative impacts on capital as well as negative effects on the agricultural production.

Agricultural machinery reduces the production cost and ensures more products. However, the taxes to be added to the machines, land or products will increase the production costs and increase the product prices. In this case, the producer with a reduction in the rate of profit stops the production. So increases in price are expected (Ricardo 2001 p. 177).

Ibn Khaldun expresses the negative effects of heavy taxes and avoiding of taxpayers to pay taxes like:

> The descendants and the tribes' being obliged to endure the payments like paying tribute, heavy fine and taxes that means indulgence and worthlessness for them constitutes the important part of this. Because none of them agree with the indulgences given by their old man and judges, none of them agree to pay these taxes, debt and tribute. Because each of these allowances is cruelty and misfortune, and the hearts who are afraid to bear the devotion can never endure this. However, as they consider them easier than being murdered, they are obliged to accept such fondness (Ibn Khaldun 1967, p. 362).

Three features of the classic model are highlighted:

Freedom: Individuals have the right to produce and modify products, labor and capital as they see fit.

Competition: Individuals have the right to compete in the production and exchange of goods and services.

Justice: The actions of individuals should be fair and honest according to the rules of society (Skousen 2007, p. 18).

The main criticism of the public sector is that the authoritarian structure of the state will not support a liberal economy.

Even though public sector and public expenditures have been assigned various tasks on economic growth, the increase in public expenditures is thought to have negative effects on economic growth (Fölster and Henrekson 1999, p. 342).

For the same level of spending and a specific budgetary function, public spending is less effective in countries with high levels of corruption. Corrupted public institutions tend to prefer the most ineffective investment projects that gives the highest bribes (Shleifer and Vishny 1993, p. 604). Corruption increases the cost of spending and reduces the amount of output provided by the state (Shleifer and Vishny 1993, p. 605).

In the same way, it is stated that public expenditures also have a negative impact on productivity. It is seen that a 10 percent increase in the total public expenditures decreased the total factor productivity growth rate by 0.92 percent. The same rate of increase in public consumption expenditures reduces total factor productivity growth rate by 1.4 percent (Hanson and Henrekson 1994, p. 390).

In Europe, debates on fiscal policy stance in terms of periodic conditions have rules on adopting the EU's fiscal rules system, which determines how to react in specific stages of economic fluctuations. Especially, in order for the medium-term budget targets to reach balanced budget positions, it is recommended that EU member states continue their financial adjustment efforts that are more ambitious economically. In times of economic slowdown, fiscal policy should be counter-cyclical. However, some critics have criticized that a 3 % ceiling over the government deficit-GDP ratio especially would slow down such effectiveness of fiscal policy (Eichengreen and Wyplosz 1998, p. 82).

However, a government's making expenditures is seen as the last way to influence economic growth. Some fiscal policy instruments can have long-term effects, but only modern internal growth models reveal public spending as the engine of economic growth (Zagler and Durnecker 2003, p. 404).

In order to ensure maximum efficiency in the economy, it is evaluated that public expenditures should not exceed 20 percent of GDP, which confirms the classical supply-oriented paradigm (Peden 1991, p. 161).

On the other hand, if the decline in income due to the decrease in the employment level goes further, consumption may only be done by some individuals and institutions and it may result in their use of their financial reserves they saved at better times. Nevertheless, the public sector may intentionally or unintentionally face a budget deficit and may have to provide unemployment benefits through borrowing. Therefore, when employment falls to a low level, total consumption will be reduced by less than the amount of real incomes, both due to the behavior of individuals and possible government policies. This is the explanation that a new equilibrium position is generally accessible in a modest fluctuation range. Otherwise, the decline in employment and income initiated once can be a sharp fall (Keynes 1936, p. 55).

However, even if the fiscal policies have expanding short-term effects, financing can be derived from private sector savings, and as a result the impact on capital accumulation can lead to a long-term decline in employment.

Weakening of Liberal Economy

The Great Depression has been seen by many as a great failure of the market economy and the concept of "Laissez faire". This failure justified government interventions, and evoked admiration for many intellectuals because of the ongoing economic problems in Russia, Germany and Italy. Following the introduction of major public expenditure programs by the United States after the crisis, it has been seen that other governments also began to make higher public spending to address the unemployment problem due to the Great Depression and to meet public needs. Beginning from the mid-1930s, military spending in response to Hitler's threat also contributed to increased public spending in European countries (Tanzi and Schuknecht 2000, p. 9).

Liberals strongly believe in individual responsibility. According to them, the state is only responsible for the protection of citizens from oppression, interference and discrimination. Hence, the state should only provide services such as police forces, courts, prisons and rehabilitation centers. The limitation of the duties of the public in this way keeps the need for public finances to a minimum (Bailey 2004, p. 7).

That is to say, the best role for the State is the "Laissez faire" model. The best thing the State can do is to withdraw from the private sector, and let them alone to do what they do best, to earn profits and income. State intervention creates a vicious circle that will arouse a need for more state intervention and incentives. Public finance remains out of control as the state increasingly seizes (i.e. taxation) revenues and wealth of the people in order to finance public spending more and more every day. Individual responsibility, on the other hand, decreases the need for public activities and encourages the private sector to grow more (Bailey 2004, p. 8). However, in some cases it can be seen that free market operation does not function properly as expected. In case of a failure in solving the problems to be solved by the free market mechanism, a need and an expectation for public intervention may occur. Such situations indicate public interventions as necessary. This is the case even in libertarian ideas.

Neo-liberal approaches, for example, just like Classical Economists, also emphasize individual responsibility. However, Neo-liberals state that there may be injustice as a result of market conditions. Because everyone cannot reach the same level of livelihood because of the differences in their ability, entrepreneurship or hard work. For this reason, the state should ensure equality of opportunity for all to achieve an adequate standard of living (Bailey 2004, p. 8).

Keynesian economists are more cautious about crises than liberal neoclassical economists. Keynesians distinguish more, deeper, and longer-term market imperfections that constantly threaten the maximization of wealth, and therefore believe that constant observation and intervene of public to overcome these imperfections and impacts. The public intervention mentioned here includes specific state policies that can shape and regulate the economic preferences of individuals and private enterprises in order to prevent, overcome or balance market imperfections (Wolf 1986, p. 63).

If free market activities do not lead to efficiency, in other words, if there is no high efficiency in the outputs, government intervention in order to increase efficiency becomes the current issue. The government can more accurately compare social benefits and social costs, as it will take into account not only the benefit and cost of a person, but the benefits and costs of all individuals as well. However, the fact that private market outcomes do not maximize efficiency does not necessarily mean that government intervention will increase productivity (Gruber 2009, p. 5).

The 1929 crisis and the legend of protectionism in depression in the 1930s led us to a more general and much more important myth about the long-term history of commercial policies. This is almost a dogma among the neo-classical economists and can be expressed like in the following terms: "Free trade is the rule, protection is the exception". How many times have we heard of the golden age of free trade since the deepening of the protectionism of the 1920s and 1930s? Historically the fact is "free trade is the exception, and protectionism is the rule (Bairoch 1993, p. 16).

The Wagner's Law (Wagner, 1883) is one of the theories that emphasize economic growth as the main determinant of public sector growth. Public expenditures are increasing due to increasing activities within the economy and increasing diversity of economic outputs. Therefore, the increase in public expenditures is an expected external factor due to economic progress (Kesavarajah 2012, p. 90).

With reference to some comments, the growth of public expenditures is faster than that of national income. That means public expenditures are flexible. According to this, a growing economy creates additional tax revenues, and political representatives create opportunities to increase public spending and state subsidies that the public will benefit from. It is seen that this increase in public sector activities continues to develop even during recession periods (Kolluri, Panik and Wahab 2000, p. 1062).

Although the literature tends to emphasize the exclusion of private investments and consumption due to financial expansion, fiscal expansion may have positive effects on the private sector. For example, state investment in physical infrastructure, such as roads, railways and ports, increases the productivity of investments for all companies and sectors and thus promotes private investments. Similarly, the providing stronger social security networks, such as unemployment benefits, can reduce the risk and uncertainty faced by households and thus lead to more consumption and less savings. Public spending may have a positive impact on private consumption and investment by increasing the confidence of consumers and the private sector in the market. This kind of confidence building effect is particularly important for violent shocks, such as the global financial crisis, with public expectations that the government is doing something to revive the economy. The larger the number of people, the greater the positive impact of financial expansion on aggregate demand and output. The net impact of a limited and medium-sized financial expansion on economic activity depends on whether or not enlargement will meet specific domestic demand or on the process (Hur, Mallick and Park 2010, p. 8).

For Keynes, uncertainty is the basis of everything. Investors complain about the human imperfections of not knowing what will happen in the future. Uncertainty confuses them when trying to calculate the expected profitability of new investments. Today's calculations are influenced by everything around them and possible future impacts. For this reason, private sector investments are expanding or receding in a rather unstable manner, as today almost all kinds of social change affect the minds and moods of investors and therefore the profit calculations. Most importantly, chaotic behavior in systems may lead the whole economy to expansion or recession (Wolff and Resnick 2012, p. 123).

These expectations for public expenditures cause the public sector to grow. For a number of developed countries, including the United States, the idea that the current level of public expenditure will remain stable at the same level as long as the state can fulfill its obligations satisfactorily. Moreover, it is expected from the State to put forward strategies to accelerate public spending and from the public sector to be effective. It is also believed that the public sector is

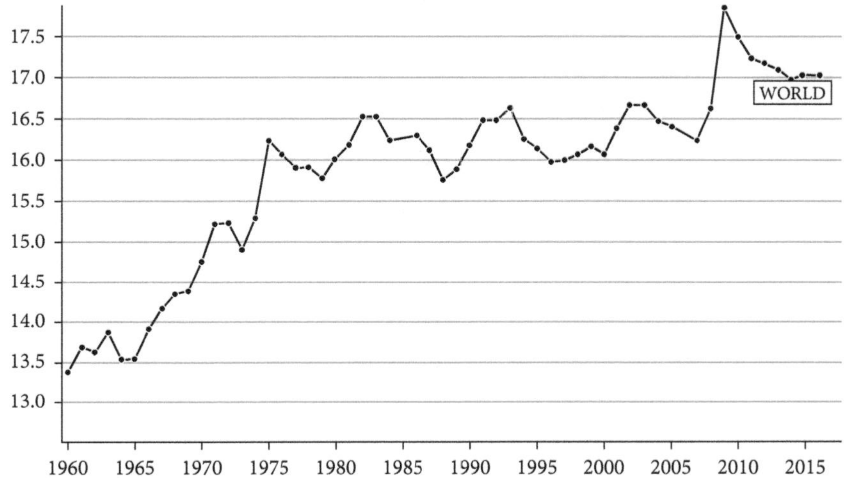

Fig. 1: World Public Spending (%of GDP, 1960–2017). Source https://data.worldbank.org/indicator/sp.urb.totl.in.zs

of vital importance to increase the efficiency of allocation of resources, especially to counteract the crises, and that maximizing the positive effects of public interventions in general is crucial as well (Florin and Bogdan, 2011).

Public spending appears to be a fact for the economy. The studies have aimed to keep it under control rather than fighting the public sector. Some changes are needed to increase efficiency in the production of public goods. First of all, the existence of bureaucracy in the production of public goods can be preserved. However, each institution should work in a competitive environment. Existing services should be allowed to be produced by other institutions and institutions should be encouraged. Dividing product or output between offices and terminating the dominance of a single office in a product or service can be effective in efficiency. Another point is that bureaucrats should be encouraged to minimize their budgets for a particular output. Also, making private and profitable organizations to do public goods and services may lead to a decrease in bureaucracy and better evaluation of the outputs (Niskanen 1968, p. 298).

The change in public expenditures in the world between 1960 and 2017 is shown in Fig. 1. According to the graphic, it is seen that the share of public expenditures in GDP increased continuously.

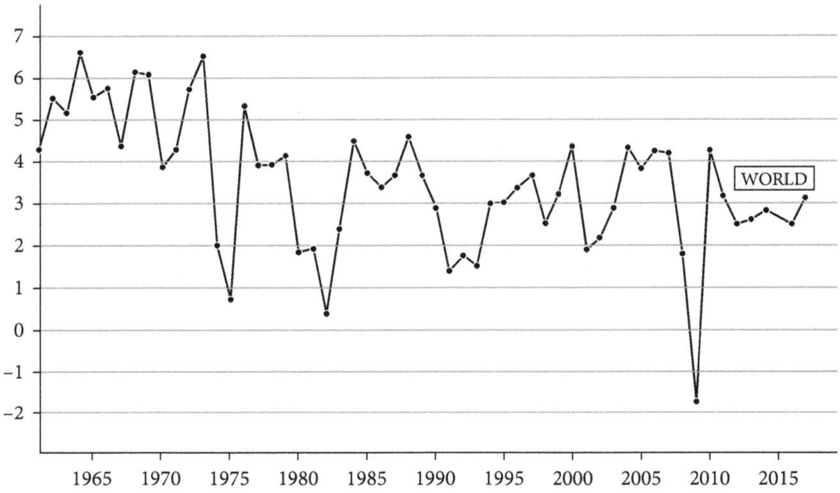

Fig. 2: Economic Growth Rate of World (%, 1960–2017). Source https://data.worldbank.org/indicator/ny.gdp.mktp.kd.zg

The growth rate of the world economy between 1960 and 2017 is shown in Fig. 2. According to the graphic, the growth rates generally had hard breaks. However, it is observed that the decreases in growth rates especially in times of crisis got stronger. Especially after the 2008 financial crisis, economic growth rates in the world had been negative for the first time since 1960.

In addition, it is seen that after the breakdowns in economic growth, the share of public expenditures in the GDP declined slightly. However, public spending rapidly rose after the crisis. After each crisis, the share of the public sector from the economy is more than its share in the pre-crisis period and it does not return to the level before the crisis. Because, it becomes very difficult to reduce it to a previous level if public spending increases once.

Conclusion

The conflict between the capital and the public sector goes back a long way. The liberal approach that gained power especially after the Industrial Revolution defend the public sector to be reduced as much as possible. It is argued that taking the resources of private sector by means of taxes by the public sector declines welfare level. The main reasons for this criticism of the public sector are the cumbersome nature of the public sector, the possibility of misuse of the state authority, the extravagant behavior of the bureaucrats, the efforts of the oppression and interest groups to benefit themselves.

However, along with the Depression of 1929, issue of trust against the free market economy began to emerge. In the early days of the crisis, the belief that free market could solve that problem had been replaced by pessimism with the long duration of the crisis. In this case, Keynes' demand-side fiscal policies had a big impact. After the crisis, it was argued that the public sector was not such a bad thing. The public sector was now in a position to solve the problem of the free market.

It is seen that this process, from the Great Depression to the oil crisis of the 1970s, was not sustainable. However, after every crisis, the public sector would be in the spotlight as the savior.

It is seen as a contradiction that capital opposes the public sector and also it expects public sector to be the savior after every economic crisis. Because public spending is reluctant to fall below its previous level. The public sector is growing after each crisis. And after each crisis, it could not return to its previous level.

In this case, the free market should develop a self-regulation system. It is recommended to pay attention to over indebtedness and to focus on green energy in order to avoid energy-related problems. Excessive risk of banking and investment should be avoided. If a task is to be assigned to the public sector, it is expected to regulate with the state authority in these areas. What is important is not to overcome the economic crisis with the help of the public sector. What is important is to ensure as much as possible that capital does not create its own crisis.

References

Bailey, Stephen: *Strategic Public Finance (First edition)*. New York: Palgrave Macmillan, 2014.

Bairoch, Paul: *Economics and World History Myths and Paradoxes (First edition)*. Chicago: The University of Chicago Press, 1993.

Dowd, Douglas: *Capitalism and its Economics a Critical History*. London: Pluto Press., 2004.

Eichengreen, Barry, and Wyplosz, Charles: "The Stability Pact: More than a Minor Nuisance?". *Economic Policy* 13(26), 1998, pp. 65–113.

Florin, Oprea, and Bogdan, Petrisor Mihail: "Public Expenditure Policy in the Context of Economic Crisis - Challenges and Implications". *Annals of Faculty of Economics University of Oradea* 1(1), 2011, pp. 416–422.

Fölster, Stefan, and Henrekson, Magnus: "Growth and the Public Sector: A Critique of the Critics". *European Journal of Political Economy* 15(2), 1999, pp. 337–358.

Gruber, Jonathan: *Public Finance and Public Policy*. New York: Worth Publishers, 2009.

Hanson, Par, and Henrekson, Magnus: "A New Framework for Testing the Effect of Government Spending on Growth and Productivity". *Public Choice* (81), 1994, pp. 381–401.

Hur, Seok-Kyun, Mallick, Sushanta, and Park, Donghyun: "Fiscal Policy and Crowding out in Developing Asia". *ADB Economics Working Paper Series* (222), 2010, pp. 1–29.

Ibn-i Khaldun: *The Muqaddimah: An Introduction to History* (trans. Franz Rosenthal), New Jersey: Princeton University Press, 1967.

Keynes, John Maynard: *The General Theory of Employment, Interest, and Money*, retrieved 22.04.2019 from. https://cas2.umkc.edu/economics/people/facultypages/kregel/courses/econ645/winter2011/generaltheory.pdf

Kesavarajah, Mayandy: "Wagner's Law in Sri Lanka: An Econometric Analysis". *Annual Research Journal of SLSAJ* (12), 2012, pp. 89–99.

Kolluri, Bharat, Panik, Michael Panik, and Wahab, Mahmoud: "Government Expenditure and Economic Growth: Evidence from G7 Countries". *Applied Economics* 32 (8), 2000, pp. 1059–1068.

Niskanen, William: "The Peculiar Economics of Bureaucracy". *The American Economic Review* 58(2), 1968, 293–305.

Peden, Edgar: "Productivity in the United States and Its Relationship to Government Activity: An Analysis of 57 Years, 1929–1986". *Public Choice* (69), 1991, pp. 153–173.

Ricardo, David: *On the Principles of Political Economy and Taxation*. Ontario: Batoche Books, 2001.

Shleifer, Andrei, and Vishny, Robert: "Corruption". *Quarterly Journal of Economics* (108), 1993, pp. 599–618.

Skousen, Mark: *The Big Three in Economics: Adam Smith, Karl Marx, and John Maynard Keynes*. New York: Sharpe, 2007.

Smith, Adam: *An Inquiry into the Nature and Causes of the Wealth of Nations*, retrieved 03.04.2019 from, https://www.era.lib.ed.ac.uk/handle/1842/1455.

Tanzi, Vito, and Schuknech Ludger: *Public Spending in the 20th Century: A Global Perspective*. Cambridge: Cambridge University Press, 2000.

Wolf, Charles Jr.: *Markets or Government: Choosing between Imperfect Alternatives*. Santa Monica: The Rand Corporation, 1986.

Wolff, Richard and Resnick, Stephen: *Contending Economic Theories: Neoclassical, Keynesian, and Marxian*. London: The MIT Press, 2012.

Zagler, Martin, and Durnecker, Georg: "Fiscal Policy and Economic Growth". *Journal of Economic Surveys* 17 (3), 2003, 397–418.

Asst. Prof. Dr. Selim DEMEZ and Prof. Dr. Zekai ÖZDEMİR

VI Theories of Monetary Crisis*[1]

Abstract: In recent years, globalization, financial liberalization and technological developments and the increasing capital movements are the most important reasons for the crises that have increased in recent years even though they provide benefits to the economies of the country in many ways. Therefore, taking lessons from the crises and understanding them is a recipe for predicting a possible crisis in the future or how to overcome a crisis. In this study, the most widespread monetary crises in the world economies are examined within the framework of the theoretical and empirical literature that emerged from past crisis experiences. Thus, it is tried to determine the macroeconomic variables that can explain and predict both the monetary crises and the monetary crises. It is also thought that this study will shed light on future studies and policy makers.

Keywords: Monetary Crisis, Globalization, Financial Liberalization

Introduction

Globalization and financial liberalization increased international capital movements by the effect of technological advancements after the 1970s. Thus, global capital can easily move from a country to another. This capital that is also called hot money is vital for countries that want to reach specific macroeconomic goals and have enough capital accumulation. Global capital generally moves to countries which are at an investable level and graded by credit rating agencies. However, hot money has a risk of suddenly abandoning the country in case of economic or political instability situations.

Under the circumstances, the economy may deteriorate suddenly. Moreover, speculative attacks on the exchange rate may damage the economy. The speculative attacks of speculators who consider the decreases in reserves of central banks in countries which adopt the fixed exchange rate cause reserves of central banks to decrease more and bring a monetary crisis at the same time. The situation that occurs in both two situations above is called a monetary crisis.

Besides such crises, banking crises arising from banks which do not fulfill their short-term liabilities can be shown as examples for frequent crises. As a matter of course, much as the key reason that drives banks to the crisis is the

---

1 This article is derived from the doctoral thesis named as 'Central Bank Monetary Aggregates' Effectiveness on Explaining the Monetary Crisis: Panel Data Analysis'

depositors who run to banks to withdraw cash because of the problems in expectations, the thing that triggers related situation is the negative course in the economy. Therefore, the monetary crisis and the banking crisis are called the twin crisis in the literature.

Any negativity in an economy may cause a possible crisis based on the fragility of the available economy. This negativity generally results from the monetary problems and affect both financial markets and the real economy. This study scrutinized the financial crises and tried to theoretically and empirically explain the monetary crises.

Crisis Concept and Economic Crises

The word crisis was derived from the word of κρίνω (krino) in Greek. Related extant word passed a great semantic shift throughout history by using in different meanings in different fields such as medicine, policy, war and religion. It is used in the political area in ancient Greek and it means decision and preference. This "preference" and "decision" reveals the choice or fact between two opposite situations. In other words, it means the choice between life and death; peace and war and right and wrong (Koselleck and Michaela 2006, p. 357).

The related word is used in meanings like "depression" today. The economic crisis is the existing scarcity and deprivation in money markets or in sectors that produce goods and services (Kibritçioğlu 2001, p. 174–175). There is a need for classifying the economic crises to deduce and understand the reasons for economic crises. As is seen below, economic crises are divided into two as the real crises and financial crises.

As is seen in Fig. 1, there are a good number of types of economic crisis. While the real sector crisis is defined as the crises that occur in product and service and labor markets, the crisis that occurs in goods and services markets is divided into two as the inflation and recession crisis. Moreover, the financial crises are analyzed under three categories as the banking crisis, currency crisis (monetary crisis) and stock market crisis. The monetary crisis is divided into two sub-categories as the balance of payments crisis and exchange rate crisis.

Real Sector Crises

These crises are demand and supply mismatches above or under equilibrium level of output in product, service and labor markets. If this situation occurs in product and service markets, it causes inflation or recession crisis; otherwise,

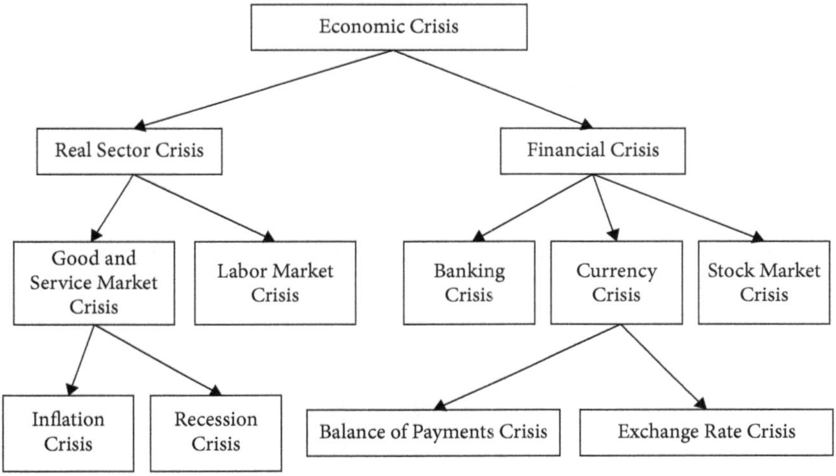

Fig. 1: Types of Economic Crises. Source: Kibritçioğlu (2001, p.180)

if the same situation occurs in the labor market, it causes labor crisis. While a demand surplus out of the available capacity or lack of supply causes inflation crisis, an opposite situation in which there is a demand insufficiency causes a recession crisis. Nonlinearities from equilibrium wage level that labor supply and demand determine in the market cause labor crises.

Financial Crises

Financial crises are the monetary bottlenecks that occur out of product, service and labor market. As is seen in Fig. 1, financial crises are analyzed under three different categories as the monetary, stock market and banking crisis. Monetary and banking crisis is called the twin crisis in the literature. Crises experiences in the past and the relationship between two crisis as cause and effect show us how much this use is to the point.

For Miskin (1996) "devaluation causes an instant increase in foreign currency liabilities of banks. Accordingly, open positions that banks try to close available resources cause a financial bottleneck; thus, there occurs a monetary and banking crisis to be experienced in the same cycle." Taylor (2009) pointed out that surpluses which occur by several reasons in an economy generally cause the monetary crises. Taylor also exemplified this situation by the last Mortgage crisis in America. Credit burden that is placed by overexpansion in the housing industry to the financial institutions results in the outbreak of a financial crisis. Thus, there is seen a global crisis that affects the developed countries first and then the whole world via selling financial instruments that are used for housing finance.

Banking Crisis

There are several definitions of the banking crisis in the literature. The most common definition is the bankrupt of banks because of the failure in fulfilling the short- and long-term liabilities; the depositors who run to banks to withdraw cash because of the problems in expectations and economy; state interventions (Hoggart, Reis, Saporta 2001, p.12–13). Banking crises have shown an increase around the world after 1970. Sixty-nine banking crises were experienced between the years of 1970 and 1996 (Altıntaş 2004, p.41). For Honahan (1997), banking crises arise because of three reasons. These reasons are the micro- and macro-economic deteriorations and the regional rises in an economic system where the public force is much. A single bank can drive an economy to the crises based on its size in the financial system.

A bank's negative expectations relating to future causes depositors to withdraw the deposits. This circumstance can be explained by the multiple equilibrium models in the research of Diamond and Dybvig (1983). With reference to the model, there are two equilibrium conditions. The first related condition is banking crisis arising from going bankrupt because of the liquidity problem that is based on the depositors who run to banks to withdraw cash because of banks' negative expectations about the future. In the second situation, expectations of depositors are positive; thus, there is no run to banks and no crisis as well (Delice 2003, p.61).

Undoubtedly that the situation above means a circumstance that is not based on the deteriorations in economic indicators. Another issue is the thought that banking crises are about the real trade cycle. Shrinkage in economic activities causes a decrease in asset prices of banks; namely, this case is a signal for depositors to withdraw the cash (Altıntaş 2004, p.42–43).

Both bank panic and trade cycle are evaluated together in studies about banking crises in the literature. Miskin (1996) focused on asymmetric information problem arising from adverse selection and moral hazard. Asymmetric information problem means repayment problem for a huge part of credits. This circumstance increases a banking crisis possibility by decreasing asset prices and net values of the companies which demand fund (Altıntaş 2004, p.43).

Currency Crisis (Monetary Crisis)

Monetary crisis means the unexpected and certain changes in exchange rate and capital movements. Related crisis is observed when the domestic currency falls in value as the result of speculative attacks and money authorities endeavor to defend the national currency by increasing the interest rates (Danışoğlu 2007, p.3). The prevailing descriptions toward monetary crisis in literature are the descriptions that are made by using decreases in real exchange rate reserves and nominal currency (Sekmen and Kürkçü 2012, p. 93).

There are several factors in arising a monetary crisis. Deteriorations in macroeconomic indicators, attacks of speculator toward domestic currency, hot money loss because of any reason cause the monetary crisis. Many empirical studies that have been conducted after 2008 crisis measure the loss in value of national currency against dollar (Sekmen and Kürkçü 2012, p. 94).

Another factor that causes a monetary crisis is that developing economies have pretty much short-term debts. This situation causes domestic currency to lose in value and economy to face with high inflation problem. Continuous depreciation of domestic currency against foreign exchange means that loans of companies which become indebted in foreign currency increase. Thus and so, many companies go bankrupt or restructure their debts in spite the high interest and currency pressure. Price instability and debt pressure that are on all the units shake the confidence to the government; a monetary crisis will become unavoidable (Doğanlar, Bal and Özmen 2007, p.271–272).

Tab. 1 shows the crises occurred after the 1990s. There are monetary crises because of excessive debt, financial problems, financial and current account deficits in countries at each development level and notably the developed countries.

Increasing monetary crises after the 1990s have attracted the attention of all experts, notably the academic community. Several theoretical and empirical studies about the issue have been conducted. It is thought that monetary crises will be understood better when related studies are analyzed.

Theoretical and Empirical Monetary Crisis Models

Various theories have been suggested to understand and avoid crises throughout history. However, no theory has been enough to fully identify and understand crises. Therefore, the common factors were systematically modeled by predicting characteristic features of crises upon. Many economic theories have been revealed to forecast the crises via macroeconomic variables and some indexes.

Tab. 1: Monetary Crises from the 1990s to Present. **Source:** Sekmen and Kürkçü, 2012, p. 92

Country	Date of Crisis	Reason for Crisis	Country	Date of Crisis	Reason for Crisis
Argentina	Feb.90	Excessive debt problem	Turkey	Mar.94	Excessive debt problem
	Feb.02	Current Account problems		Feb.01	Financial problems
Iceland	Oct.08	Excessive debt problem	Sweden	Nov.92	Excessive debt problem
Brazil	Nov.90	Excessive debt problem	Mexico	Dec.94	Financial problems
	Oct.91	Excessive debt problem	Venezuela	May.94	Fiscal deficits
	Jan.99	Financial problems		Dec.95	Fiscal deficits
Colombia	Aug.95	Financial problems	Norway	Dec.92	Fiscal deficits
	Sep.97	Current Account problems		Jul.98	Excessive debt problem
	Sep.98	Financial problems		Jul.99	Excessive debt problem
	Aug.99	Financial problems		Nov.00	Excessive debt problem
Denmark	Aug.93	Excessive debt problem	Philippines	Dec.97	Excessive debt problem
Finland	Nov.91	Excessive debt problem	Spain	Sep.92	Financial problems
	Sep.92	Excessive debt problem		May.93	Financial problems
Greece	Nov.09	Excessive debt problem	Portugal	Jan.10	Excessive debt problem
Indonesia	Dec.97	Excessive debt problem	Thailand	Jul.97	Excessive debt problem
	Jan.98	Excessive debt problem		Jan.98	Excessive debt problem
Malaysia	Aug.97	Financial problems		Sep.99	Excessive debt problem
	Aug.98	Financial problems		Jul.00	Fiscal deficits

Accordingly, empirical crisis theories toward estimate and understand crises took place in the literature. Financial crises consist of monetary and banking crises and generally arising from monetary reasons. Since this study scrutinized the monetary crises, this chapter focused on monetary crises theories.

Monetary Crisis Theories

Monetary crisis theories are divided into two as the theoretical and empirical crises theories. With reference to the first generation models, deteriorations in economic indicators and incorrect economy policies cause monetary crises. The second generation models point out that speculative attacks of speculators toward foreign exchange expectations have an essential role in crises. The third generation models focus on the probability of spreading monetary crises, behaviors of intermediary institutions and moral hazard problem. Empirical monetary crisis theories are the studies that are conducted in any country or country groups. The chief goal is to determine what the proper macroeconomic variables are to forecast or explain the crises.

Theoretical Monetary Crisis Models

Theoretical monetary crisis models are the theories which endeavor to explain why crisis arise by analyzing political and economic changes in the national economy before and after the crises. Especially the developing countries can direct the economic policy in light of these models. Such models are the advisors to be preserved from crises in unexpected time.

The First Generation Monetary Crisis Theory

It is the monetary crisis model that gained a theoretical framework by being developed in the article of Flood and Garber (1984). The related model was revealed in Krugman's (1979) study toward explaining the crises in Mexico in 1973–1982 and Argentina in 1978–1981. Krugman's model is based on Salant and Henderson's (1978) study in which they tested behaviors of people who keep gold by speculation motive in the case of stability authorities aspire to buy and sell gold at a certain level.

This study assumes that speculators will keep hold of a product based on their expectations toward increasing the relative price of the product; otherwise, they will sell the related product out. Speculators making buying and selling decision by making a comparison between a shadow price and the price that is determined by stability authority. Speculators sell the related product out by thinking that they will not earn more if the price of the product is at or over the shadow price level. In the exact opposite situation, they repurchase because of the thought that the price of the product will increase in the future. Undoubtedly that this situation decreases the available reserves. From this point of view, the first generation monetary crisis models that were revealed by Krugman (1979) and developed in the article of Flood and Garber (1984) arose by adding effects of being sold foreign exchange by the Central Bank to provide financial stability against speculative attacks.

This model that is also called the Canonic crisis model emphasizes that financing the public deficits by emission and internal borrowing in the fixed exchange rate system causes a currency crisis. In other words, efforts to keep the exchange rate at a certain level against the increase in money supply of the Central Bank cause a decrease in foreign exchange reserves; thus, the speculative attacks for the increasing foreign exchange demand causes a fixed exchange rate to be abandoned and reserves to deplete faster (Flood and Garber, 1984, p. 4). Being sold foreign currency to the market by the Central Bank to meet the increasing foreign currency demand causes reserves to get to deplete; a monetary crisis becomes unavoidable because of the speculative attacks. The first generation monetary crisis models clarify that a monetary crisis stems from the disharmony between monetary policy of monetary authorities and exchange rate policies (Durmuş 2010, p. 35).

Complaints about the model are as follows: the model is mechanic and routinized; being introduced foreign currency by monetary policy authorities of the country, efforts of monetary policy authorities to try to explain monetary crises by foreign exchange reserve and budget deficits (Durmuş 2010, p. 35). The related model remains incapable to clarify the European Exchange Rate Mechanism (ERM) in 1992. This is because the second generation monetary crisis theories were suggested.

Extended First Generation Model

This is a model that was revealed by the study of Agenor, Bhandari and Flood (1991) and Flood, Garber and Kramer (1996). The bond market is also affected by the increase in policy interest rates as the result of the demand for money authority to want to meet the speculative attacks to the exchange rate by sterilization policy. There is observed an expansion in domestic credit level; thus the scissors between the foreign interest rate and domestic interest rate by adding a risk premium to the difference between the foreign interest rate and domestic interest rate. Under these circumstances, money authority starts to sell the foreign bond to the market by sterilization policy; the amount of bonds of the private sector increases at the end of the process. Accordingly, money supply and money demand which are aimed by the money authority demand can be controlled (Çeviş, 2005 p. 38). This is a new model that arose by adding a risk premium to the interest rates.

Second Generation Monetary Crisis Theory

The second generation monetary crisis models are the models that are established on the thought that positions of economic units against positive-negative expectations about future invalidate the economic policies of the monetary policymakers. In other words, acquainted speculators get the position based on the foresight that whether monetary policy and reserves of the Central Bank are sufficient against the speculative attacks. A related position is a theory which reveals that a situation that arises from speculative attacks and is called self-fulfilling expectation may cause the crisis (Doğanlar, Bal and Özmen 2007, p. 261).

On the other hand, even though the economic program that is conducted by money authorities about the current economic situation is consistent, the change in expectations may cause a monetary crisis in an economy under the influence of speculative attacks in spite of a stable economic situation (Doğanlar, Bal and Özmen 2007, p. 261). However, Jeanne (1997) expressed that it is impossible for self-fulfilling expectations to create a crisis alone; negative signals in main macroeconomic indicators may cause a self-fulfilling crisis by bringing exchange rate to an unsustainable level (Jeanne 1997, p. 267).

The second generation monetary crisis theory was first revealed by Obsfeld (1986). Afterward, Obsfeld (1994 and 1996) developed the model more via his studies. Multiple equilibria were added to this model besides the self-fulfilling expectations. Kenen (1996) exemplified this issue as follows: three possible situations come into question when it is assumed that two identical account owners have separate unit of national currency and these owners completely know the number of reserves in the Central Bank.

i) The situation in which the Central Bank has high reserves (R>2n): There is no speculative attack. Because the acquainted account owners know that the speculative attacks toward foreign currency will fail.

ii) The situation in which the Central Bank has low reserves (R<n): A speculative attack in this situation is inevitable. Because both two account owners know that their personal attacks produce results.

iii) The situation in which the Central Bank has reserve at midlevel (2n>R>n): Speculative attack is no inevitable in this scenario. Arising a

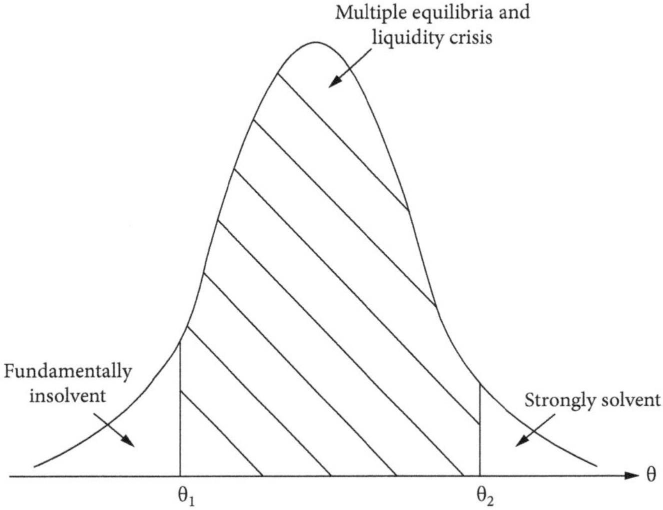

Fig. 2: Relationship Between Economic Magnitudes and Multiple Equilibrium.
Source: Chui et al. (2000, p. 369)

speculative attack is based on the expectations of both two account owners. Because an attack of a single speculator is not big as much as giving rise to a change in the exchange rate.

As is mentioned above, there is a multiple equilibrium system. Sustainability of exchange rate is evaluated by the Central Bank based on the expectations of speculators (Kenen 1996, p. 473). It is seen when this three scenario are evaluated that 2n>R>n completely reveals the subject of the second generation monetary crisis theory. Determination of money authorities in applying the fixed exchange rate is crucial. Fig. 2 transparently shows the relationship between macroeconomic indicators and multiple equilibria in the first and second generation crises.

In Fig. 2, θ shows the economic magnitudes; the area that is at the left side of θ_1 represents the area where economy is in a financial difficulty; the area that is at the right side of θ_2 represents the area where expectations and economic indicators are good; the area in the middle shows the area where economy is open to crisis that is based on self-fulfilling expectations. The area in the middle also shows the area that is generated by multiple equilibrium. The area that is at the left side of θ_1 shows the area where the ability, namely the macroeconomic indicators are low. When viewed from this aspect, economy may face a crisis that is explained in the first generation crisis model in this area. Economy does not face a crisis at the right side of θ_2. This circumstance does not mean there will be no crisis; the issue should be considered within the frame of multiple equilibrium (Emirmahmutoğlu 2011, p. 25).

Third Generation Monetary Crisis Theory

The third generation crisis theories arose because of remaining incapable of the first and second generation crisis models to forecast and explain the crises in the Far East Asian countries in 1997 and 1998. This model that was developed by Krugman (1998, 1999) and he argues that the moral hazard problem that arises from being government's guarantor for external debts of the private sector is the key reason for the crisis. Being issued guarantee for credit back payments by the government in Far East Asia causes financial institutions to finance unprofitable investments; this circumstance also brings about credit volume growth. Moreover, repayment problems that arise in credits which cannot be directed to profitable investments have caused governments to lose big capitals.

For Krugman, the banking system and contagion effect are crucial in monetary crises in the third generation models. While the factors such as asymmetric information problem, adverse selection, moral hazard and audit weakness have an active role in the part that is about banking system, contagion effect is spreading a crisis from a country to another one just as an epidemic (Krazner 2004, p.7–8).

The third generation crisis models can be analyzed under three main titles:

- Financing risky investments arising from the moral hazard problem of banks renders the fixed rate system unsustainable,
- Collapsing occurs in financial markets by self-fulfilling speculative attacks toward financial markets in outward-oriented economies, banks panic,
- Decreasing items in balance sheet arising from devaluation that occur by passing from the fixed rate system to flexible exchange rate (Krugman 2001, p. 3–7)

Indeed, the banking crisis and the monetary crisis play an efficient role in modeling the third generation crises. This situation is called twin crisis in the article of Kaminsky and Reinhart (1999). Twin crises emphasize that monetary and banking crises are interrelated. In the broadest sense, a crisis that arises in the banking sector because of reasons above causes a monetary crisis via interest channel; monetary crisis brings about deepening the banking crisis. Especially the twin crises show themselves in cases in which financial fragility is high and economic indicators worsen (Kaminsky and Reinhart, 1999, p. 474).

Empirical Crisis Theories

Foreseeing and explaining the crises are tested by empirical analyses; related analyses can determine the variables at the same time. Analysis of early warning signal models, restricted dependent regression models, crisis intensity model and continued crisis model with two regimes can be seen in this chapter.

Early Warning Signal Models

Financial globalization means sharing risks and advantages at an international level in terms of markets. Globalization and integration of financial markets that started after 1980 have made developing the financial market system open to the crisis threat (Öz and Taban 2007, p. 2).

Importance of early warning signal models has increased by the effect of monetary crises in the 1990s. The necessity of specifying leading indicators on behalf of estimating crises with shrinking economies by Europe Currency system Crisis, Mexico Crisis, Asia Crisis and Russia Crisis, macroeconomic indicators that are negatively affected and financial markets that lost their trust. The early warning system is important in terms of taking proactive measures and making required observations during the crisis. The early warning system has a limited usage area because of the lack of data required for running this observer mechanism in a proper way (Altıntaş and Öz 2007, p. 20). Early warning signal model can provide projection only by estimating data via empirical models.

There have been conducted several studies on the early warning signal models. Following studies contributed to the literature; Eichengreen, Rose, and Wyplosz (1995), Kaminsky, Lizondo and Reinhart (1997), Berg and Pattillo (1998), Kaminsky (2000) and Edison (2000). Related studies have pioneered for the next academic publishings.

Eichengreen, Rose and Wyplosz (1995)

Eichengreen, Rose and Wyplosz (1995) conducted a study about estimating monetary crises by the early warning signal model and sought answers for below questions that are difficult to understand for policy makers:

- Are there significant differences between economic and political variables so as to cover the periods with crisis and without crisis?
- Have policymakers economic and political moves to protect their national currency from speculative attacks?
- Are there significant differences between authorities' methods such as protecting the currency, devaluating and floating based on political variables after a speculative attack?
- How should policymakers manage the unclearness in currency markets?

The course of economic and political variables is crucial in terms of the foreign exchange market. Moreover, political moves of authorities determine the future of their own currency.

Eichengreen, Rose and Wyplosz (1995) aimed to analyze the monetary crisis by speculative attack measurement that is developed by excluding devaluation and fluctuations arising from crisis environments including unsuccessful speculative attacks. They compared available devaluations and other variables in exchange rate arrangements. They used an index that is obtained from interest rate differences, the weighted mean of change in the exchange rate and changes in international reserves against speculative pressures as the crisis variable. The analysis was conducted by collecting data of 24 OECD member countries. With reference to the research results, capital control in developed countries decreases the monetary crisis possibility (Wyplosz 2001, p. 254). A similar study was performed by Rossi (1999) for developing countries; the same result as the study of Eichengreen, Rose and Wyplosz (1995) was obtained.

Eichengreen, Rose and Wyplosz (1995) pointed out that noising reform call around by a louder noise in the international monetary system is not an undue concern to tide over. They also emphasized that the exchange rate is essential for macroeconomic balance; re-regulation is significant for eliminating the imbalances that are frequently seen in macroeconomic basics. In addition to all these, changes in the foreign exchange regime are in a weak relationship with the macroeconomic indicators in contrast to the re-regulation (Eichengreen, Rose and Wyplosz 1995, p. 300).

Kaminsky, Lizondo and Reinhart (1997)

The process that follows the collapse of currencies of some Asian countries as from the beginning of 1997 July has been discussed by academic studies to research the reasons for monetary crises. The issue of predictability of monetary crises by the governments brought about the question marks.

Kaminsky, Lizondo and Reinhart scrutinized the issue of whether there is a functionality between the early warning system and the monetary crises in IMF's report in March of 1998. Running the early warning signal system in a proper way and required indicators are crucial to avoid the monetary crises and solve the economic problems. Being systematically displayed different behaviors by some of the indicators before the crisis took a signal task to avoid the crises. Three data group can be seen if the macroeconomic indicators are classified (Kaminsky, Lizondo and Reinhart 1998, p. 9):

- Capital Account: This data group includes the data such as international reserves, capital flows, short-term foreign capital investments, domestic and foreign interest rates.
- Debit Account: Public external debt, total external debt, short-term liability, debt ratio based on the type of creditor specific to the structure of interest, debt services and foreign aid.
- Current Account: Real exchange rate, current account balance, trade equilibrium, export, import, terms of trade, export prices, savings and investments.

Variables within the frame of analysis cover the main data that can reflect all macroeconomic basics of a country.

Early warning signal model is also known as the 'signal model' as well as it is a system that measures the crisis possibility after the warning signal of the macroeconomic data. Variables like international reserves, real exchange rate, domestic lending, credits for the public sector and domestic inflation rate give significantly good results before the crisis. Again the variables such as trade balance, export performance, monetary expansion, real GDP increase and fiscal deficit support the pre-crisis early warning signal (Kaminsky, Lizondo and Reinhart 1998, p. 24). Other indicators are characterized as the uncertain or indefinite signal transmitters as the result of empirical analysis.

Berg and Pattillo (1998)

There were also performed comparative studies about the development of the early warning signal model. Those studies that are fed by the same issue and fact aim to estimate the pre-crisis period by measuring the sensitivity of specific indicators to the crisis.

The 1994 and 1997 crises and other crises that arose in 1997 give a perfect chance to test the early warning signal model. The 1997 Asian crisis provides a special area for the investigators about struggling with the crisis. Investigators notice when researching the reasons for the crisis that the related reasons are at macroeconomic and structural dimension rather than being traditional microeconomic bases. Poor banking supervisions, weak corporate and bribery are the most important reasons for this crisis. On the other hand, the Mexican Crisis in 1994 has been an inspiration to various studies.

Sachs (1997) argues that the characteristics of the crisis in Thailand in 1997 is similar to the Mexican crisis in 1994. With reference to the research, reasons such as overvaluation of real exchange rate, intense tendency to the housing sector and multiplying bank debts are the key factors that trigger the Thailand crisis. In other respects, each crisis brings along new characteristics and findings. Berg and Pattillo (1998) prefer to restructure KLR (1997). Although they found similar results in the analysis that was conducted for 20 countries between the years of 1970 and 1995, the effect of some of the indicators remain weak. For KLR study, while 12 indicators have an effect that can enlighten the issue, solely 8 indicators take the signal task in the related research (Berg and Pattillo 1998, p. 129). Berg and Pattillo emphasized that structural problems come into prominence besides variables that are tested for early warning system model in financial crisis experiences.

Kaminsky (2000)

Banking crises have started to rise to prominence in the economic field as from the midst of the 1980s. Problems about banking system gradually increase from the time till today; prevent stabilization of currency and increase the intensity of monetary crises. Although financial fragilities are more frequently seen in developing countries such as Mexico between the years of 1992 and 1996, Thailand in 1996 and Indonesia in 1997, developed countries like Japan has not got rid of this problem. Moreover, the aggregation tendency of monetary and banking crises caused them to be called a twin crisis (Kaminsky 2000, p. 2). Twin crisis concept is more effective by intense economic activities in terms of all the countries.

We can say when looking at the issue as result-oriented that monetary and banking crises are not the new facts. Costs of financial crises are high. IMF foresees that there are 4 %–7 % cumulative output loss in monetary crises. Banking crises increased this ratio to 12 %. Effect of twin crisis is bigger; its financial obligations may be bigger as well. Just as in examples of Chile and Argentina in the early 1980s, related costs may occur above 40 % of GDP in some instances. Financial problems are about reserve losses in monetary crises. The Central Banks undergo a difficult process to keep the exchange as the result of expired initiatives (Kaminsky 2000, p. 22).

Kaminsky's (2000) study have first step characteristics for performing early warning system. It is thought that there are effects of various indicators within the scope of the early warning system. Accordingly, it is suggested to develop an early warning system in line with a common dataset consists of M2 multiplier, the ratio of domestic credits to GDP, domestic real interest rates, the ratio of M2 to reserves, export, import and terms of trade.

In general terms, fragility for crises has increased by developing financial markets and financial globalization. It can be focused on the tendency of neighboring countries to crisis while the macroeconomic bases are evaluated. Therefore, reviewing the early warning system in a narrower area is a remarkable handicap for the crisis to signal early.

Discussing the indicators that represent a balance of payments problems while the indicators in a macroeconomic basis are tested within the early warning system is important for foreseeing the crises. There is a thought that a new early warning system can be developed by taking the model of Kaminsky and Reinhart (1999) a step further and also by inserting banking and private capital flows. While the increasing financial sector fragility triggers the economic recession, worsening public finance characterized the pre-crisis period. Foreign bank credit inflows increase in pre-crisis periods. Increased domestic credits increase the possibility of financial markets to be exposed to crises. Almost all monetary crises follow the banking crisis. Recent studies pointed out that a banking crisis increases the monetary crisis possibility by 9,6 % (Lange 2013, p. 35).

Edison (2000)

An early warning system that is called the system that defines precautions in the pre-crisis period came to exist on the purpose of minimizing the costs in a crisis environment.

Early warning system approach focuses on behaviors of specified indicators in a situation independent of a crisis. Classifying while choosing the indicators just as Edison (2000) will ease the analysis. A model-data group to forecast a crisis can be established by reviewing variables such as deviation in real exchange rate, balance of payment including import and export data, foreign exchange reserves, M2/foreign exchange reserves, capital account including differences of domestic and foreign interest rate on deposits, share price index, real sector data including industrial production with M2 multiplier, domestic credits/nominal GDP, real deposit rate, real M1 balance surplus, deposits of commercial banks.

Performance of the early warning system has a complex structure. This system may cause false alarm in the pre-crisis period as well as it varies country by country. It is argued based on this information that easy money policies and losses in foreign exchange reserves cause a monetary crisis. Moreover, economic shrinkages in the world's leading markets like the United States of America and G7 countries when the international economic relationships are considered (Edison 2000, p. 7–40).

Restricted Dependent Regression Models

Crisis models are classified to be explained. Related classifications are as follows:

- The First Generation Models (Canonic): As is called by Krugman, the first generation models emphasize that budget deficits cause financial crises. Financing budget deficits by coining damages the exchange rate system and makes the economy open to speculative attacks as the result of the losses in foreign exchange reserves (Durmuş 2010, p. 32).
- The Second Generation Models: These models emerged by the reason of canonic crises models to remain incapable to explain European Monetary System Crisis and 1994 Mexican Crisis. Negative expectations that are brought by negative economic conditions establish the reason for the crisis. This concept is modeled cost-benefit analyses and negative expectations in the market by the policymakers (Çakmak 2007, p. 10).
- The Third Generation Models: One of the most remarkable problems that come into prominence in this crisis model is the moral hazard problem. The problems of the financial sector rather than speculative attacks are reviewed in this modeling. Asymmetric information and moral hazard in financial markets establish the reason for crisis (Sevim 2012, p. 37).

While the first of the empirical models to explain the monetary crisis models is the early warning system, another one is the restricted regression models.

Following studies can be exemplified for the studies that endeavor to explain the restricted dependent regression models (Frankel and Rose (1996), Eichengreen, Rose and Wyplosz (1996), Esqivel and Larrin (1998), Kruger, Osakwe and Page (1998)):

Frankel and Rose (1996)

Answering below questions will be beneficial while discussing the monetary crises (Frankel and Rose 1996, p. 351):

- Do the monetary crises in developing countries emerge as a result of the same political mistakes?

- Are these monetary crises the result of unfortunate shocks?
- Can monetary crises be estimated by standard economic indicators?
- Can different countries similarly react in post-crisis period? Do political reactions change by country or time?
- Are all monetary crises the same?

Several programs are organized by the IMF to continuously control the finance and macroeconomic performances of the countries. More than 800 fund regulation was performed for 132 countries by stand-by agreements during 40-years from 1952 to 1992. Besides industrial societies, developing countries benefit from these sources as well (Santaella 1995, p. 1). Hundreds of regulations and fund transfers aimed to avoid monetary problems in line with developed international economic relations.

Monetary crises are in the tendency to arise in northern countries when reserves decrease; domestic credit volume is increased; foreign direct investments are withdrawn based on the overvaluation of real foreign exchange rates. The interesting situation here is that neither budget deficits nor the balance of payments disequilibrium signal for a typical crisis (Frankel and Rose 1996, p. 365). As is understood from this circumstance, leading indicators that specify the crisis in terms of northern countries may vary by other countries. This is because it is possible to obtain statistically more significant results by using part and region restriction while the leading indicators of the crisis are analyzed.

Eichengreen, Rose and Wyplosz (1996)

It is thought that speculative attacks have a partial correlation with the crises. Therefore, authorities should also query whether monetary crises have a contagious feature for other countries as the result of speculative attacks. Commercial ties between countries which are in close international economic relations cause monetary crises to create similar results on the macroeconomic variables.

Whether the monetary crises have a contagious character can be tested for countries for specific years. Study of Eichengreen, Rose and Wyplosz (1996) about this issue is a vital reference. The study is based on the hypothesis that findings that are statistically and economically significant are contagious. They argued that any monetary crisis anywhere in the world increases a monetary crisis possibility by 8 % in other countries. On the other hand, high inflation and unemployment rates at the macroeconomic dimension increase the speculative attack possibility as well. When viewed from this aspect, a speculative attack in another country of the world increases the speculative attack possibility against the currency of a related country.

Esquivel and Larrain (1998)

Investigators may conduct empirical studies with several variables in line with the opportunities of theoretical background. Therefore, studies should be performed by classifying countries based on their development level, geographical positions and their roles in international economic integration. For example, a situation that is valid for developing countries may not be valid for developed countries. Under these circumstances, developed and developing countries need to be evaluated between each other in the empirical analysis.

Esquivel and Larrain (1998) looked for answers for the crisis environment that involves many countries of Asia and Mexico.

Every investigator can develop new expressions while there is made definitions of monetary crises. This issue is completely about the perspective that is utilized for commenting on the monetary crises. Unsuccessful speculative attacks were excluded from the new model developed. There is focused on the collapse of the exchange rate system from a different viewpoint. Explanatory variables that are used to model the monetary crisis based on the content of the model are as follows:

- Seniorage that shows the annual change of reserve money through a percentage of GDP
- Overvaluation or irregularity of real exchange rate
- Balance of payments
- Ratio of M2 money supply to reserves
- Shocks of international terms of trade
- Increase in per capita income

Various expectations are created for models to be the reasons for monetary crises while they are used in the model. The more successful a country is, the lower the risk of exposure to the monetary crisis. In another case, it expected from seniorage data to be directly proportionate to monetary crisis possibility. Because, for Krugman, old monetary crises are seniorage-driven (Esquivel and Larrain 1998, p. 16–20).

It is possible to estimate the crisis in line with the behaviors of variables that are utilized in the model. The possible crisis situation can be estimated in terms of both developing and developed countries including an early warning system.

Kruger, Osakwe and Page (1998)

There is a need for answering two main questions in monetary crises in terms of developing countries. Related questions are as follows:

- Do monetary crises have a relation with the bases of the economy?
- Is there any evidence relating to the contagiousness of monetary crises in the following stage after controlling the effects of the bases of the economy?

Indicators that describe developing countries or transition economies as macroeconomic are selected in similar characteristics. Analysis difference here consists of periodical and regional data scope. Namely, the ability of some of the indicators to estimate crisis may change because of different country groups and different period reviews. Kruger, Osakwe and Page (1998) conducted statistical research about the predictability of monetary crises by using variables below:

- External debt/GDP
- M_2/reserves
- Current accounts deficit/GDP
- Public fiscal deficit/GDP
- Growth rate of domestic loans
- Rate of per capita income growth
- Receivables of banks from private sector/GDP
- Consumer price index inflation rate
- Real exchange rate
- Foreign interest rate

Related variables represent the macroeconomic bases of an economy, and they are known as the factors that are most affected by the monetary crises.

Regionally contagiousness of monetary crises is significant at a high level. A monetary crisis in a neighboring country increases the possibility of a speculative attack against the currency of the related country by 8,5 %. In conclusion, excessively increasing credits, deviations from the real foreign exchange rate and reserve deficit mean the monetary system of an economy becomes open to speculative attacks. Contagiousness of monetary crises can be clearly seen when spreading of Thailand crisis to Indonesia, Philippines, Malaysia and South Korea is considered (Kruger, Osakwe and Page 1998, p. 16).

Crisis Intensity Model

Crisis intensity represents a different mathematical model that was developed for explaining the monetary crises. The studies by Sachs, Tornell, and Velasco (1996), Corsetti, Pasetti and Roubini (1998) and Cartapanis, Dropsy and Mametz (2002) contributed to literature about this issue.

Sachs, Tornell and Velasco 1996

Mexican crisis has characteristics of an experience that provides to be taken required measures in terms of the monetary crises. Monetary crisis in Mexico emerged as the result of unreasonable financial behaviors in contrast to crises in Latin America. Since the budget balance has a surplus in the period of 1990–1994, the problem does not originate in macroeconomic bases of Mexica. The financial risk level of Mexico establishes the main reason for the crisis. There are three factors that cause investors to beware:

- Urgent short-term liabilities (especially the public debt in the dollar),
- Collapsing the banking system as the result of booming trade payables,
- A spiral collapse in the foreign exchange rate.

Mexico became addicted to external debts in early 1993 and 1994. The balance-of-payments deficit was almost about 8 % of GDP in 1994. It's no secret that there is a fragile structure in the financial system. However, there is a need for following the policies of the government about liquid assets and responsibilities to understand the source of the panic in Mexica. Consequently, the reason for the panic is the government of Mexica that loses its trust. Short-term liabilities can be associated with two factors. These related factors are deepening and liberalization of the capital (Sachs, Tornell and Velasco 1995, p. 14–18).

Especially continuing the capital inflows including debt/GDP, portfolio and foreign direct investments whose economic relations deepened in 1994 came into prominence. It is seen that the function of automatic regulator mechanisms under a fixed exchange rate regime has become difficult by increasing interest rates of the US if the over values Peso is considered (Sachs, Tornell and Velasco 1995, p. 14–18). Accordingly, the floating rate regime became compulsory.

Economies that experienced an increase in credits are inclined to monetary crises. Countries which are defenseless to inverted capital inflows have a poor banking system, overvalues real exchange rate and low reserves relating to liquid liabilities. Variables in the related model reflect this circumstance. Below variables are the main reasons for the financial crises when there is conducted an analysis by the selected country groups:

- Real Exchange Rate
- Credit Boom (Extreme raises in the short term)
- M_2/Reserves

Although there are capital inflows by any reason, loss in value remains under the beginner level if a country has a strong banking system and a standard exchange rate.

This situation causes investors to run away and the economy is balanced at the same time. In other words, an economy which is built on a strong foundation is resistant to speculative attacks. Similarly, there will be no speculative attack if economy which is built on a weak foundation but M2/Reserve ratio is low. As a conclusion, the crisis that is based on speculation arises in periods when both the foundations of economy and reserves are low (Sachs, Tornell and Velasco 1996, p. 163).

Corsetti, Pesenti and Roubini (1998)

With reference to expressions, financial crises arising from speculative attacks to currencies in the 1990s arose as the result of financial and monetary instabilities.

Corsetti Pesenti and Roubini (1998) endeavor to determine the Asian Crisis by the help of several indexes and modeling peculiar to themselves.

- Crisis index: Weighted mean of losses in the real exchange rate in US dollar represents the crisis index.
- Financial fragility index: This represents the credits of banks for the private sector between the years of 1990 and 1996. This index is also known as the increases in credit rates.
- Current account imbalance index: This index is calculated by expressing current account balance through GDP. This index that is expected to be more than a specific starting point is mistaken for the real exchange rate losses.
- Foreign reserve deficiencies and key performance index of the economy: The possibility of being experienced monetary crises increases if the reserves are low. Three main indicators are used as a base about this index. These indicators are M1/foreign reserves, M2 foreign reserves and external debt burden.

Inherent and main weaknesses within the real and financial sector deepen the monetary crisis possibility. External disequilibrium can successfully explain the crisis index. Fragility is high in countries with low reserves; for authorities, those economies are more indurable against crises (Corsetti Pesenti and Roubini 1998:13).

Cartapanis, Dropsy and Mametz (2002)

Cartapanis Dropsy and Mametz (2002) pointed out when analyzing the Asian Crisis that although related countries were on a successful line in the last thirty years in the pre-crisis period, they have an insecure economic environment against the attacks. While previous studies generally analyzed based on the first generation crisis modelings, they scrutinized crisis in three parts: instability, insecurity and contagiousness.

Monetary crisis index is established when the data are specified in the first stage of the empirical analysis. The index is determined through international reserves and the real effective rate of exchange for each of the countries. The model is purified from movements by selecting the real effective rate of exchange. The analysis is conducted via stock and flow variables by using variables like financial imbalances and external shocks to represent macroeconomic instability and financial insecurity. Macroeconomic variables that are selected in accordance with this purpose are as follows (Cartapanis, Dropsy and Mametz 2002, pp. 82–84):

- Real effective exchange rate in terms of showing overvaluation in currency,
- Current account balance/GDP in terms of representing external disequilibrium,
- Public budget balance/GDP as an indicator of financial imbalance,
- The ratio of long-term investments/GDP growth rate in terms of showing imbalances in the banking system,
- External debt, real foreign exchange rate and capital flows in terms of showing the external shocks.

Asian Crisis must not be evaluated as only the overvaluation of currencies. Asian crisis is the most important evidence that monetary crises are contagious. It should be remembered when a new global financial structure is built that monetary crises may splatter from country to country (Cartapanis, Dropsy and Mametz 2002, p. 90).

Continued Crisis Model with Two Regimes

Vlaar (2000) separately reviewed crises as the off-peak period and crisis period in the model with two regimes. Crisis index in this study shows continuity as well as it is also based on international reserve loss or depleting the reserves. Observations provide information about monetary mistrust in periods when the economy is depressed. This mistrust and deficits arise by two crisis regime at first. The second regime shows high fluctuation and substantially shrinkage. Definition of crisis periods is the result of stochastic processes except for restricted dependent models. Countries with strong foundations face high exchange rate volatility.

Crises are partially predictable. However, adding political factors to the model in terms of some of the countries causes being obtained more significant results from the model. Therefore, there is a need for adding a dummy variable that shows a political risk factor to the model in countries with political problems and high sensitivity.

Conclusion

Almost all the economies in the world face economic crises in specific periods by internal or external factors. Recovering economy after the crisis takes time and negatively affects the welfare level of economic units. Forecasting crises are vital for policymakers. Because a possible crisis is a situation that can be struggled via traditional economy policies based on crisis intensity. Estimating crises is possible by determining the type of crises by deteriorations in macroeconomic data. Crisis experiences of the past bring light to policymakers in modeling the economic situation. This study aimed to draw a framework for monetary crises by the studies of experts and economists. It is thought that this study will provide a theoretical framework for the next studies.

References

Altıntaş, Halil: "Bankacılık krizleri, nedenleri ve ekonomik maliyetleri". *Erciyes Üniversitesi İktisadi ve İdari Bilimler Fakültesi Dergisi* (22), 2004, pp. 39–61.

Altıntaş, Halil and Öz, Bülent: "Para Krizlerinin Sinyal Yaklaşımı ile Öngörülebilirliği: Türkiye Uygulaması". *Anadolu Üniversitesi Sosyal Bilimler Dergisi* 7 (2), 2007, pp.19–44.

Berg, Andrew and Catherine Pattillo: "Are Currency Crises Predictable? A Test". *IMF Staff Papers* 46 (2), 1999, pp. 107–138.

Cartapanis, André, Vincent Dropsy, and Sophie Mametz: "The Asian Currency Crises: Vulnerability, Contagion, or Unsustainability". *Review of International Economics* 10 (1), 2002, pp. 79–91.

Chui, Michael KF, Prasanna Gai, and Andrew Haldane: "International Financial Crises and Public Policy: Some Welfare Analysis". *Bank of England Quarterly Bulletin*, 2000, pp.368–376.

Corsetti, Giancarlo, Paolo Pesenti, and Nouriel Roubini: *Fundamental Determinants of the Asian Crisis: A Preliminary Empirical Assessment.* Unpublished manuscript (New Haven, New York, New York: Yale University and University of Bologna, Federal Reserve Bank of New York and NBER), 1998.

Corsetti, Giancarlo, Paolo Pesenti, and Nouriel Roubini: "Paper tigers? A Model of the Asian Crisis". *European Economic Review* 7 (43), 1999, pp.1211–1236.

Çakmak, Umut: "Para krizi modellerine ilişkin bir değerlendirme". *Ekonomik Yaklaşım* 18 (62), 2007, pp.1–31.

Çeviş, İsmail: *Para krizlerine ampirik bir yaklaşım*. İstanbul: Sermaye Piyasası Kurulu, 2005.

Danışoğlu, Ayşe Ç: "Para Krizleri: Türkiye'de Yaşanmış Krizlerin Değerlendirilmesi." *Sosyal Bilimler Dergisi* (2), 2007, pp. 1–11.

Delice, Güven: "Finansal Krizler: Teorik ve Tarihsel Bir Perspektif." *Erciyes Üniversitesi İktisadi ve İdari Bilimler Fakültesi Dergisi* (20), 2003, pp. 57–81.

Doğanlar, Murat, Harun Bal, and Mehmet Özmen: "Döviz Krizi Modelleri." *Journal of the Cukurova University Institute of Social Sciences* 16(1), 2007, pp. 253–276.

Durmuş, Savaş: "Finansal Krizleri Açıklamaya Yönelik Yaklaşımlar", *Kafkas Üniversitesi Sosyal Bilimler Enstitü Dergisi* 1(5), 2010, pp. 31–46.

Edison, Hali J: "Do Indicators of Financial Crises Work? An Evaluation of an Early Warning System." *International Journal of Finance & Economics* 8(1), 2003, pp.11–53.

Eichengreen, Barry, Andrew K. Rose, and Charles Wyplosz: "Exchange Market Mayhem: The Antecedents and Aftermath of Speculative Attacks." *Economic policy* 10(21), 1995, pp.249–312.

Eichengreen, Barry, Andrew K. Rose, and Charles Wyplosz: "Contagious Currency Crises". *National Bureau of Economic Research Working Paper Series* (5681), 1996, pp. 1–50.

Emirmahmutoğlu, F. "Gelişmekte olan ülkelerde para krizlerinin ekonometrik analizi." *Gazi Üniversitesi Sosyal Bilimler Enstitüsü Ekonometri Anabilim Dalı, Yayınlanmamış Doktora Tezi,* Ankara, 2011.

Esquivel, Gerardo, and Felipe Larrain. "Explaining Currency Crises." *John F. Kennedy Faculty Research WP Series R98-07*, 1998, p. 42.

Flood, Robert P., and Peter M. Garber: "Collapsing Exchange-Rate Regimes: Some Linear Examples." *Journal of International Economics* 17(1–2), 1984, pp. 1–13.

Frankel, Jeffrey A., and Andrew K. Rose: "Currency Crashes in Emerging Markets: An Empirical Treatment." *Journal of International Economics* 41 (3–4), 1996, pp. 351–366.

Hoggarth, Glenn, Ricardo Reis, and Victoria Saporta: "Costs of Banking System Instability: Some Empirical Evidence". *EFA 2001 Barcelona Meetings, Bank of England Working Paper* (144), 2001, p.38.

Honohan, Patrick: "Banking System Failures in Developing and Transition Countries: Diagnosis and Predictions". *BIS Working Papers* ISSN 1020-0959, 1997, p. 50.

Jeanne, Olivier: "Are Currency Crises Self-Fulfilling? A Test." *Journal of International Economics* 43(3–4), 1997, pp. 263–286.

Kaminsky, Graciela, Saul Lizondo, and Carmen M. Reinhart: "Leading Indicators of Currency Crises." *Staff Papers* 45(1), 1998, pp. 1–48.

Kaminsky, Graciela L., and Carmen M. Reinhart: "The Twin Crises: The Causes of Banking and Balance-of-Payments Problems". *American Economic Review* 89(3), 1999, pp. 473–500.

Kaminsky, Graciela Laura: "Currency and Banking Crises: The Early Warnings of Distress". *IMF Working Paper* (178), 1999, pp. 37.

Kenen, Peter B. "Analyzing and Managing Exchange-Rate Crises." *Open Economies Review* 7(1), 1996, pp. 469–492.

Kibritçioğlu, Aykut: "Türkiyerde Ekonomik Krizler ve Hükümetler, 1969–2001". *Yeni Türkiye Dergisi Ekonomik Kriz Özel Sayısı* 1(41), 2001, pp.174–182.

Koselleck, Reinhart, and Michaela W. Richter: "Crisis." *Journal of the History of Ideas* 67(2), 2006, pp. 357–400.

Kruger, Mark, Patrick N. Osakwe, and Jennifer Page: Fundamentals, Contagion and Currency Crises: An Empirical Analysis, *Bank of Canada* 98(10), 1998, p. 29.

Krugman, Paul: "A Model of Balance-of-Payments Crises." *Journal of Money, Credit and Banking* 11(3), 1979, pp. 311–325.

Krugman, Paul: "Crises: The Next Generation." *Conference Honoring Assaf Razin, Tel Aviv*, 2001, pp.27

Krugman, Paul: "Balance Sheets, the Transfer Problem, and Financial Crises." *International Finance and Financial Crises*. Springer: Dordrecht, 1999

Krznar, Ivo: "*Currency crisis: Theory and practice with application to Croatia*". *Crotia National Bank Working Papers*, (12), 2004, pp.46.

Lange, Ronald H: "Monetary policy reactions and the exchange rate: a regime-switching structural VAR for Canada." *International Review of Applied Economics* 27(5), 2013, pp. 612–632.

Mishkin, Frederic S: "*Understanding financial crises: a developing country perspective*". *National Bureau of Economic Research Working Paper Series* (5600), 1996, pp. 1–40.

Obstfeld, Maurice: "Rational and self-fulfilling balance-of-payments crises.", The American Economic Review 1(76), 1984, pp. 72–81.

Obstfeld, Maurice: *The logic of currency crises Monetary and fiscal policy in an integrated Europe*. Berlin, Heidelberg: Springer, 1988.

Obstfeld, Maurice: "Models of currency crises with self-fulfilling features.", *European economic review* 40(3–5), 1996, pp. 1037–1047.

Oz, Bulent, and Sami Taban: "Türkiye'deki Para Krizlerinin Reel Değişkenlerle Sinyal Yaklaşımıyla Öngörülebilirliği". *Beykent Üniversitesi Sosyal Bilimler Dergisi* (1), 2007, pp.1–28.

Sachs, Jeffrey, Aaron Tornell, and Andres Velasco: "*Financial crises in emerging markets: the lessons from 1995*". *National bureau of economic research* (5576), 1996, pp.147–215.

Sachs, Jeffrey, Aaron Tornell, and Andres Velasco. "The collapse of the Mexican peso: what have we learned?" *Economic policy* 11(22), 1996, 13–63.

Salant, Stephen W., and Dale W. Henderson: "Market anticipations of government policies and the price of gold." *Journal of political economy* 86(4), 1978, pp. 627–648.

Santaella, Julio A: "Four decades of Fund arrangements: Macroeconomic stylized facts before the adjustment programs", *International Monetary Fund*, 1995.

Sekmen, F., Kürkçü, M: "Küreselleşen Dünya'da para Krizi Olgusu", *Finans Politik ve Ekonomik Yorumlar* 49(573), 2012, pp. 89–102.

Sevim, Cüneyt: *Öncü Göstergeler Yaklaşımına Göre Finansal Krizler ve Türkiye Örneği*. Ankara, BDDK Kitapları No:11, ISBN: 978-975-9004-15-6, 2012, pp. 252.

Taylor, John B: "The financial crisis and the policy responses: An empirical analysis of what went wrong". *National Bureau of Economic Research*, (14631), 2009, pp.1–2.

Vlaar, Peter JG.: *Currency crisis models for emerging markets*. Amsterdam: De Nederlandsche Bank NV, 2000

Wyplosz, Charles. "How risky is financial liberalization in the developing countries?." *Comparative Economic Studies* 44(2–3), 2002, pp. 1–26.

Assist. Prof. Dr. İhsan Seddar Kaynar

VII Turkey's First Devaluation: 7 September 1946 Decisions

Abstract: Turkey's first devaluation of 7th September Decisions is one of the most important economic events in the Turkish economic history in 1946. Turkey's foreign trade partners were defeated in the Second World War (WW2). Therefore, her foreign trade opportunities in the postwar period had narrowed. After WW2, the new order began to be established, pioneered by the United States, and in order to participate in this order, Turkey needed to make a number of changes. In this study, Turkey's first devaluation of 7th September Decisions will be examined, with a focus on state' expectations from the decision and the practical consequences of the devaluation. The Republican Archives, Parliamentary Papers, Resmi Gazete and Cumhuriyet and Ulus newspapers, which were published in September 1946, are used.

Keywords: Devaluation, Monetary Crisis, Turkey, Ration, 1946

Introduction

The problem of money, which was inherited from the Ottoman Empire to the Republic of Turkey, began in 1914 with the start of the First World War (WW1). Paper money, which was printed in 1915, continuously depreciated until 1929 (Aral 1944, pp. 260–272). Government had took various measures since 1929, and these measures were merged together by the Law no. 1567 enacted on 15 February 1930 (Resmi Gazete 25 February, 1930). Turkish lira for the gold cover was abandoned and the value of one sterling was accepted as 1.030 kuruş. Turkish currency indirectly linked to the gold by means of sterling. However, devaluation of sterling came in September 1931, and Turkey chose the French franc as the base currency. However, France abandoned the gold standard in 1936, and Turkish currency lost her convertibility.

Turkish Government stated in an official regulation that the Turkish lira would continue to be the gold equivalent on 26 September 1936. This relative system did not continue much and the WW2 began in 1939. With the Law no. 3974 dating 6 January, 1941, the Turkish currency was officially relinked to sterling (Resmi Gazete 15 January, 1941). One sterling officially started to be sold from 520 kuruş and bought from 524 kuruş at Central Bank of the Republic of Turkey. However, sterling had different values in the money market depending on the type of operation. After 1939, there happened no interference to the value of the Turkish currency until 7 September 1946.

There are usually two reasons for devaluation of money (Suvla 1948, p.1). The first reason is to stabilize the money if the value of money is decreasing, while losing the ability of money to turn into gold. The second reason is to eliminate the constraints of export, i.e. to overcome the economic crisis. Before the devaluation of 7th September, there were two important examples of devaluation in the world, one in United Kingdom and the other one in the United States. The sterling was devalued in the UK in 1931, and in the United States in 1933. In the UK, it aimed to increase exports without raising domestic prices; in the United States, domestic prices were aimed to be increased and exports were given a secondary importance (Suvla 1948, p.3). However, by means of devaluation, Turkey aimed the expansion of the export quantity, and intended to increase the price of the export goods.

The devaluations of the UK and the US were made before the WW2 and various policy sets were supported. After a massive capital escape from the UK, which caused the devaluation on 21 September 1931, the UK left the gold standards. The sterling lost about 40 percent of its value. The Great Depression of 1929 affected the US most. Roosevelt, who became President in 1932, announced a development plan called the New Deal, which included the devaluation of 1933. It was made in order to increase production by increasing prices, to prevent unemployment and make dollar competitive with sterling. The dollar was devalued three times in the year of 1933 and lots of laws were enacted to support the economy (Suvla 1948, p. 9).

The Stages of Decisions

The Democrat Party, who would rule Turkey between 1950 and 1960, was founded on 7 January 1946. Turkey's first multi-party general election was made on 21 July 1946 in the political history of Turkey. The Republican People's Party (CHP) received the majority of votes. Although the ruling party had not changed, the 1946 election was the first phase of the institutionalization of democracy. Ankara Deputy İsmet İnönü was elected as the president on 5 August 1946 (Resmi Gazete 6 August, 1946). Within a few days, the first cabinet of the multi-party period started to work under the chairmanship of Recep Peker (Resmi Gazete 8 August, 1946). The government's program was read and accepted in the Parliament on 14 August (Resmi Gazete 15 August, 1946).

There was no sign of devaluation in the CHP's electoral program and even in the newly established Government's program. The 7 September Decisions were adopted in the Assembly Group of the CHP, which was the ruling party till 1950. It was not a decision of the Cabinet or a law of the Parliament. After the general election, on 7 September, it was in line with the decisions of the Government in the CHP Assembly Group. The 7 September Decisions were a set of policy practices consisted of the regulations of the Central Bank of the Republic of Turkey and the Ministry of Commerce. The Government led the process of the 7 September Decisions and devaluated the Turkish lira on the base of the Law on the Protection of the Value of Turkish Currency.

The CHP took **four decisions** in the Parliamentary Group on Saturday, 7 September. In order to reestablish the economic equilibrium that has been spoiled by the war years, it was necessary to regulate the economy around a price level appropriate to the country and world conditions in order to increase production and imports. The government would like to create free market by getting rid of artificial methods in foreign trade such as clearing and barter. According to the principles of Breton Woods, it was necessary to reach government's target of being able to participate to the world trade with a sound structure and normal methods (Ulus 8 September, 1946). It would be ensured that the low price of the export goods would establish reasonable price levels and make exportation of products easy, which were not sold due to the high prices. Thus, the exports would be increased and the imports would be expanded. On the basis of these reasons, the Government adopted the following decisions by the CHP Assembly Group:

1 Currency premium system [prim] were abolished. Parity should be determined according to internal and external realities.
2 It aimed to increase the people's living conditions and to let the imports of non-luxury goods out. Moreover, government should allocate exchange to imports, determining the price of imported goods without waiting for export price to meet the imports.
3 The general level of prices should be reduced by means of decreasing the input prices of the industrial and forest products, and transportation tariffs.
4 In preparation for the Bretton Woods agreement, the government wanted to ensure the development of international trade, and a respectful monetary system, which would be established by the United Nations.

The Central Bank of the Republic of Turkey adjusted the exchange rates for various currencies on the basis of Article 37 of its laws in line with the government's decision (Cumhuriyet, 8 September, 1946). On 9 September, the new rates which were set by the bank for dollar, sterling, Swedish krona, Swiss franc and Egyptian pound would have started to be applied. 1 dollar would be bought from 280 kuruş and sold at 282,80 kuruş. 1 Sterling would be bought from 1128.40 kuruş and sold from 1139.68 kuruş, as the government terminated the premium system.

The Ministry of Commerce took **seven measures** to expand imports.

1 The new exchange rates would encourage exports and the country's foreign exchange income would increase. Foreign currency would be allocated to imports without waiting for these currencies to arrive.
2 Quantity restrictions such as plafon and quota were removed in import policy.
3 The variety, quality and price controls determined by the importers assembly were finished.
4 If the terms of the delivery have been exceeded or other conditions have not been fulfilled, the letters of credit opened up to this day, which were granted the right of recourse, would be allowed to change with other goods included in the import list.
5 The application process of import permit requests would be facilitated and the acquisition would be accelerated.
6 Importers would decide whether the goods were needed for market or not.
7 The detailed explanations of the above decisions could be obtained from the offices of the Ministry on Monday, 9 September, 1946.

The Ministry of Customs and Monopolies took two decisions to implement the decisions of September 7 to the customs. These decisions were based on the exchanges taken before September 7 and the values of the goods introduced into the country since 8 September.

The Ziraat Bank started gold trade which had a great impact on commodity prices. One gram of gold was bought from 4,50 and started to be sold at 4,545. After the war, the sale of gold in the market was liberalized (Cumhuriyet 9 September, 1946).

A Quick Glance at Turkish Economy

Turkish foreign trade was carried out with the gold standard until WW1 that destroyed lots of countries. Debts, disruption of payments and budget deficit disrupted the gold standard. After the WW1, clearing and private barter system were preferred and continued until WW2. In the clearing system, it was essential that money was removed and that countries mutually change their commodities with commodities. Turkey ensured the continuity of foreign trade without damaging the price fluctuations in the world, as she also preferred the clearing system. However WW2, which started in 1939, destroyed the European economic structure and caused a deadly blow to the clearing system. It was seen that the international foreign trade system began to deteriorate since 1914 and this problem was tried to be solved before the war ended in 1944. Bretton Woods agreements were prepared and "International Monetary Fund" (IMF) and "World Bank" were established. The IMF accepted the definite payment system based on gold or money that had a certain value, not merely the clearing principle. It was decided that to have a certain value for each dollar or under US dollar with 0,888671 grams of gold. It appears that after WW2, the world tended to abandon the clearing system. While Turkey was entering Bretton Woods's system, she was no longer possible to continue the clearing system. However Turkey's monetary system had a big obstacle to enter this system. In order to do foreign trade in Bretton Woods's system, Turkish currency should be convertible into the currencies of the other countries.

It was not realistic to compare the price level of Turkey before 1946 with world prices because of the clearing system. At the end of the WW2, there was 346 percent increase in the wholesale prices and 231–54 percent increase in living expenses compared to 1938 in Turkey. This meant that domestic prices increased by 3–4 times and the purchasing power of Turkish lira decreased significantly. While the war increased domestic prices of Turkey, it also increased the prices in other countries as well. With the exception of defeated countries' economies price levels did not rise as much as Turkey. The increase in the wholesale prices of countries increased by 35 percent in the United States, 70 percent in the UK and 100 percent in Switzerland from 1938 to 1946. Living expenses increased by 28 percent in the United States, 30 percent in the UK and 51 percent in Switzerland. When compared with foreign countries, the increase was about 1 in 10 in Turkey. Purchasing power in Turkey decreased by 350 percent, which was 30 percent higher than in foreign countries. Approximately 40–50 percent of the difference was reduced by the premium system applied in foreign trade.

The comparison of the exchange rate of the Turkish lira with the dollar before and after the war can make the situation clear. One dollar was 129 kuruş in 1938, while on the eve of 7th September, to 40 percent premium 180.60 kuruş, and 48 percent premium 190.92 kuruş in 1946. Purchased at 129 lira in 1938, the price of the goods increased with more than 346 percent and purchased at 575 lira in 1946 in Turkey. In 1938, the goods purchased in the US with 100 dollars in 1946 with 35 percent more than 135 dollar was taken. This is 257,74 lira in 48 percent premium rate. These two goods were at the same price in 1938, but it was 575 kuruş in Turkey and 257 kuruş the United States in 1946. Turkish domestic purchase decreased by 346 percent, while foreign purchases fell by 100 percent (with 48 percent premium).

As a complementary regulation of 7th September Decisions, the exchange rates and Turkish lira premium system were removed. Before the decisions, there were three different prices as official price, exporter price and importer price. The official price applied to ordinary citizens, and 1 dollar was equal to 129 kuruş in 1946. For the exporters of the foreign currency, 1 dollar was 180.60 kuruş from the price of selling goods abroad, 40 percent of the premium price of the high price of the Turkish lira. The importers paid a 48 percent premium of 190,92 kuruş for one dollar, for the price of the goods they brought from outside. These differences were abolished on 7 September and the price of 1 dollar was fixed at 280 kuruş and the selling price was fixed at 282.80 kuruş. The premium procedure was removed for the exporters and importers. The value of the Turkish currency was reduced vis-a-vis foreign currencies. The decisions adopted on 7 September 1946 were recorded as the first official devaluation of the Republic of Turkey. The devaluation of the Turkish lira was 117 percent without premium, 55 percent according to 40 percent premium rate and 46.6 percent according to 48 percent premium rate.

This was the first time in the history of Turkey that its money lost so much of its value. Then, it was necessary to prevent negative comments in the public. Therefore, the ruling party prepared leaflets and sent them to the CHP Regional Inspectors. These propaganda document was aimed to eliminate the negative impact of the decisions (State Archives, 6-33-5). As all the cabinet members were the member of the CHP, it took decisions that as it felt the need to explain and defend these decisions to her local organizations. Hilmi Uran's signature was seen on the official documents of the CHP (State Archives, 6-33-5). Hilmi Uran was the chairman of the Parliamentary Group, where the decisions were taken. He did not mention the September 7 Decisions in his memoirs written ten years later. Moreover, he wrote different stories about his re-election as a member of the parliament in 21 July, 1946. Once, he said that he was resting outside of Ankara by the end of September (Uran 1959, p.461).

Most importantly, lots of goods were derationed one by one after the devaluation. First good was bread that derationed by telegram. Bread distribution offices under the control of municipalities founded during the WW2 (Cumhuriyet 10 September, 1946). These offices were closed after devaluation. From the 9th September morning, bread was derationed. Gold trade had also became free especially for dentists and goldsmiths (Ulus 9 September, 1946). Government decided to take new decisions that tea and coffee would be derationed till November (Ulus 10 September, 1946).

The First Effects of Devaluation

Commodity prices increased **for fold** in Turkey because of the inflation that occurred during WW2. The exchange rates set fixed at a lower level, domestic and external purchasing power of Turkish lira diverged each other. Since 1930, the foreign exchange had been kept under strict control and foreign trade had been largely done by clearing. The first results of the Devaluation of 1946 were seen in four aspects (State Archives, 6-33-5):

1 **Exports:** The exchange rates for export goods increased by 44 percent. This means a 44 percent increase in prices. It was clear that this increase would be more. However, there was a scarcity of import goods in the country for 6 years. The goods were already sold at black market prices. After the September 7 Decisions, it was possible to buy these goods. A car tire, which was 3000 Sterling on the black market, was then being sold for 250 Sterling officially. The pre-war level of car tire price was 170 Sterling.
The same situation could be observed in the trucks. Second hand truck sales, which cost 25–30 thousand Sterling, of were then left behind. Trucks prices ranged between 7500 and 10,000 Sterling. The number of who bought trucks was already over 800. Truck's owner number was a typical example, because it showed the increase in the transportation capacity of the country.
Light bulb, rubber, tin, fountain pen, razor, toothbrush and comb had been on the black market or some factories went to bankruptcy. However, after devaluation, the black market immediately ended, prices became cheaper than in the past. The 44 percent increase started to become normal, abundance and competition made it more acceptable in comparison to world prices.
Abundance of goods resulting from devaluation would eliminate the costs.

2 **Imports**: The 7 September Decisions were important for the benefit of the Turkish people's needs and wants. Seventy-five percent of the Turkish import goods consisted of tobacco, grape, fig and hazelnut. Domestic sales of these products did not exceed 10 percent. The increase in prices of these products did not increase the cost of living.

3 **Domestic Goods:** For the price increases of these goods, we need to look at agricultural products. Quantity and quality of them also depended on the season and weather conditions. For example if we looked at prices in Ankara and Istanbul, the situation became clearer.
The price of one kg lamb was 140 kuruş in November 1945, and still 140 kuruş in 1947 in Ankara. The price of bread was 30 kuruş and still daily bread rations were set in November 1945, and was 25 kuruş and already derationing in 1947.

Flour was rationed and it was 60 kuruş in 1945. It was 38,5 kuruş when flour rationing ended in 1947. The price of Ghee was 450–500 kuruş in 1945, and was 550/600 kuruş in 1947.

The olive oil, which caused a lot of complaints due to its high price in the last years and therefore distributed on the ration book, was then 245 kuruş. White cheese was 210–220 kuruş in the last year; that year it was 185–210 kuruş. While the cheapest olive was 120 kuruş in the past years, it was 110 kuruş that year. Egg prices were 8.5–9 kuruş, chicken prices were 250–300 kuruş and they were same as the last year. There was no change in the prices of pasta (71 kuruş), sugar (185 kuruş), milk (60 kuruş), wood (6,5 kuruş) and coal (17,5 kuruş).

These products were 80 percent of the cost of each family. The prices of bean and dried fruits, which were allowed to be exported, were increasing. The price of bean was 78 kuruş last year, but increased to 85 kuruş in 1946. However, lentil and chickpea prices were falling. Lentils were 65–70 kuruş, then it was 50–65 kuruş. The chickpea fell from 55–70 kuruş to 55–62.5 kuruş.

Istanbul wholesale prices index, which was calculated on the 146 commodities sold in Istanbul, decreased by 10.7 percent on average from September 1945 to September 1946.

4 **Textiles and Clothing:** Prices in the textile sector had not increased, or even declined. The exchange rate difference incurred the loss of the black market trader. Some traders, who earned 100–150 kuruş from 1 meter of printing, were no longer able to win it after September 7 Decisions. Plenty of foreign exchange was allocated to the market. This lowered the prices with the fear of future goods.

The black satin fabric used by the tailors was 850–1000 kuruş on the black market, after the 15 days from 7 September Decisions, the official importer price became 455 kuruş, and it was sold to the end user at 560–700 kurus and wholesale price was 550 kurus.

Decisions Caused Delays in Investment

After the general election of 1946, the Turkish Grand National Assembly (TBMM) was opened on 1 November 1946. The MP Ahmet Oğuz submitted a parliamentary questionnaire about the devaluation on 19 September, 1946. Minister of Finance Halit Nazmi Keşmir gave a verbal reply to this question on 13 November, 1946 (Tutanak Dergisi 13, Kasım, 1946). The minister orally responded these ten questions on behalf of the Government. Initially, the debate between the minister and the MP took 3 hours with the participation of other deputies. Prime Minister Recep Peker could not stand the debate, and finished this conversation.

During the war years, domestic prices increased by 4 times. In other words, the Turkish lira depreciated in the domestic market. The external market value was unbalanced by the measures taken. In order to normalize the economy, an adjustment had to be made. The general level of post-war prices entered a downward trend, the signs of narrowing in the market and the scarcity of foreign money caused to a halt in export. As a result of these, government made 7 September Decisions, which was though urgent. After September 7, there was a 55 percent increase in the cost of imported goods and a 48 percent increase in transport costs, while workers' wages and taxes also increased. In fact, in the contracts prepared at the end of 1945 and early 1946, it was taken into consideration that market prices tended to be cheaper as WW2 was recently ended. In the course of the war, the price base was accepted, the fixed price contracts was signed in short-term jobs. The long-term jobs were considered as a protective measure as they took into account the price decreases only after the contracts and rejected any price increase. The fact that the state devaluated national money by 44 percent in one night was an unpredictable situation in the contracts. Considering that price changes increased the inflation indirectly, it was seen that there were conditions that make it difficult for contractors to do business. After the decisions of 7th September, some contractors declared that they could not fulfill their commitments due to extraordinary increases in the prices of material and labor. Moreover, they decided to look for a legal ground and sue the State. It should be noted that the decline in the value of the Turkish lira and the uncontrolled change in the prices indirectly increased the inflation. It was seen that the economic process constituted the conditions that made it difficult for the contractors to do business. We found 3 different cases in the state archives.

In Narlı-Gaziantep Line, Ankara Medical Faculty Buildings, and 7th part of Elazığ-Van Line contractors stopped the works on the construction due to 7 September Decisions (State Archives 251-21-1). The trial process started in May 1948, and the cases were seen by the Ankara Commercial Court of First Instance. When the new price determinations were made, different cost rates were estimated as 44-44-34-33 percent. Turkish Government was represented by Sadık Arda, as the legal counsel of the ministry (State Archives, 170-28-4). The Government did her best to win these cases, and sent Sadık Arda to Switzerland and prepared an important expert review of the September 7th Decisions. Prof. Egger, who lived in Switzerland, submitted his review to the court. On the other hand, the contractors was informed by the Ministry to start and to complete their works. It was understood that the contractors gave a break on purpose, and they were hoping to win the case. Although the Ministry submitted a new price offer, they did not accept it. The price difference offered by the Ministry was seen insufficient, and the contracts were terminated after a while by the government. The construction of Narlı-Gaziantep Line did not start and no progress was made.

The contracts which were signed in 1946 were terminated by the Ministry on 20 September 1948. Government made a tender three times for Narlı-Gaziantep Line. As the prices did not change in all tenders, no one was willing to sign the contract. The increase in the rates found by experts were 27.11 percent to 51 percent. This situation was recorded as unpredictable and it was concluded that the Ministry was not a defect. Contractor of different parts of Narlı-Gaziantep Line filed a petition and offered peace with government (State Archives 251-21-1).

While the case was in progress, the Ministry agreed to give extra allocation to provide a price difference for the materials received from abroad. Although this difference was not accepted, contractors decided to liquidate the work. However the liquidation conditions were not accepted by the High Council. This time, the contractors claimed that the price increase was unpredictable. They sued the Government. Finally, the contracts were terminated by notification. In the end, the General Assembly of the High Council resolved the dispute between the two parties by coming to an agreement for damages arising from the termination of contracts. Third Chamber of the High Council decided to compromise on 3 July 1955 (State Archives 255-5-16).

Conclusion

Turkey's 7th September Decisions solved the monetary problems by replacing foreign trade regime completely with a new one. In accordance with the free market conditions, price and quantity restrictions were removed. On 9th September, when the decisions began to be implemented, bread was derationed. Then, one of the most iconic rationing practices of WW2, ended in Istanbul, Ankara and Izmir. Gold trading was released. Moreover, it was announced that grain transportation was released from October. After these decisions, Import Assembly also stopped working as a government agency.

Devaluation was made to prevent the increase of Turkey's exports and was preferred losing the value of the money. Turkey abandoned the method of clearing and started to use money. A couple of months later, Turkey included in the Bretton Woods Agreement and became a member of the IMF on 11 March 11 1947. WW2 did not lead to economic problems, as WW1, the process of establishment of the IMF was initiated in Bretton Woods. The victorious states set up the IMF's fund to support each other in terms of monetary policy and free trade.

Devaluation was announced when 80 percent of Turkey's foreign trade was based on barter which was made with Germany. The export prices of the agricultural products, purchased by the state until September 1946, increased by the devaluation. Devaluation was tried to be adopted as a policy to the interest of exporters. In practice, it was resulted to the benefit of farmers, at the expense of industrialists. Devaluation was discussed at the Second Congress of Economics in Turkey in 1948. The paper on Foreign Trade Regime, which was prepared by the Istanbul Merchant Association, gave wide coverage to the 7 September Decisions among the others issues (Kılıçdaroğlu 1948, p.341). The liberalization in foreign trade, which started on September 7, was seen dangerous and the government was thought to regulate foreign trade by taking measures. It is understood that traders preferred the Sterling, not the dollar due to the high prices in foreign trade.

Exports increased by 64 percent in 7 months following the devaluation. It was lower than expected. Import restrictions were removed and imports were doubled as foreign exchange was allocated to the market. These import goods were industrial substances, fuel oil and some raw materials. In the middle of 1947, the exports exceeded the imports. Turkey's foreign currency and gold stock decreased by 22 percent in one year. Prices of export goods increased between 20 percent and then 70 percent. The only product whose quantity increased after devaluation was tobacco. However, before the war, tobacco was sold to Germany. After the war, it looked for new markets to be sought.

Seventh September Decisions are the measures taken by Turkey to join free market after WW2 and to adapt to the new economic policy that were implemented in the world (Tuna, 2007). The aim is to increase the exports by removing the price and quantity constraints on foreign trade, and through limited increase in imports, lowering the price of export products in Dollars (Kepenek and Yentürk 2001, p.118). However, in the following period, foreign trade gave continuous deficit and imports increased more than exports. Turkey's external debt was 356 million lira in 1945, 703 million lira at the end of 1949, and 6210 million lira at the end of 1960 (Kepenek and Yentürk 2001, p.119). The deteriorated structure of foreign trade created a crisis that required a second devaluation on 4 August 1958. Gülten Kazgan reckons four large and damaging crisis of Turkish Economy, respectively in 1929, 1958, 1978, and 1999–2001 (Kazgan 2005, p.1). In the first three cases, the problem of foreign debt was encountered and the last one was overcome with the support of the IMF. The

1958 and 1978 crises followed by the deepening of a political crisis and a military coup in 1960. The first debt agreement with the IMF came on 1 January 1961, when the President Cemal Gürsel signed the first stand-by agreement.

Prime Minister and Minister of Finance defended the decisions in Ulus newspaper on 8 September as such: A price regulation was made in accordance with the world's conditions. (Ulus 8, September, 1946). Turkey should have to participate in world trade by accepting the principles of free exchange and competition, and to comply with the principles of Bretton Woods. As the prices were high, we expected that with the export of new products, in the new export season, the price increases would be reflected on the producers and this would affect the increase in imports. It was known that these views, which followed a very theoretical approach, were largely based on Neumark's report. Neumark was a faculty member of Istanbul University, who took refuge to Turkey from Nazi Germany. He wrote a report on the request of the Central Bank of the Republic of Turkey's Istanbul Branch Manager about Turkey's economic policy after the WW2. He suggested the establishment of an income tax scheme like the German type. Neumark claimed that his views were used by Recep Peker in defending the devaluation (Neumark 2008, pp.241–242). Neumark became more visible in an article he wrote to Cumhuriyet on 11 September 1946 (Cumhuriyet, 11 September, 1946).

Decisions of September 7 was the first earthquake of Turkey's shift to US block. Niyazi Berkes states that by means of devaluation, Turkey economically left the Nazi economic sphere and started to convert to American economy (Berkes 2019, pp.383–386). This is the most concrete explanation of both the timing and content of decisions. Von Papen and Saraçoğlu signed lots of friendship, trade and credit agreements; these were clear evidences for Germany's influence on Turkey during the war period. Germany was Turkey's largest trade partner and prices was determined by clearing agreements, which made it difficult to determine the monetary value of the trade vis-a-vis the other currencies of the world.

References

Aral, Namık Zeki: Dünya Paraları ve Bizim Paramız, In: *Türkiye Ekonomisinin Başlıca Meseleleri*, Ankara: Türk İktisat Cemiyeti Yayınları, 1944.

Berkes, Niyazi: *Unutulan Yıllar*, İstanbul: İletişim Yayınları, 2019.

Cumhuriyet, 8 September, 1946

Cumhuriyet, 9 September, 1946

Cumhuriyet, 10 September, 1946

Cumhuriyet, 11 September, 1946

Kazgan, Gülten: *Türkiye Ekonomisinde Krizler*. İstanbul: İstanbul Bilgi Üniversitesi Yayınları, 2005.

Kepenek, Yakup and Yentürk, Nurhan: *Türkiye Ekonomisi*. İstanbul: Remzi Kitabevi, 2001.

Kılıçdaroğlu, Kemal: *1948 Türkiye İktisat Kongresi 22–27 Kasım 1948*. Ankara: Devlet Planlama Teşkilatı Yayın ve Temsil Dairesi Başkanlığı Yayın ve Basım Şube Müdürlüğü, 1997.

Neumark, Fritz: *Boğaziçi'ne Sığınanlar*. İstanbul: Neden Kitap, 2008.

Resmi Gazete, 25 February 1930, Sayı: 6378

Resmi Gazete, 15 January 1941, Sayı: 6380

Resmi Gazete, 6 August 1946, Sayı: 6386

Resmi Gazete, 8 August 1946, Sayı: 1433

Resmi Gazete, 15 August 1946, Sayı: 4708

State Archives of the Prime Ministry of the Republic of Turkey, Fonds of Republican Period, (BCA) 6-33-5.

State Archives of the Prime Ministry of the Republic of Turkey, Fonds of Republican Period, (BCA) 170-28-4.

State Archives of the Prime Ministry of the Republic of Turkey, Fonds of Republican Period, (BCA) 255-5-16

State Archives of the Prime Ministry of the Republic of Turkey, Fonds of Republican Period, (BCA) 251-21-1.

Suvla, Refii Şükrü: *Devalüasyon ve Tatbikatı*. İstanbul: İsmail Akgün Matbaası, 1948.

TBMM Tutanak Dergisi, 13.11.1946

Tuna, Serkan: Cumhuriyet Ekonomisinin İlk Devalüasyonu: 7 Eylül 1946, *Akdeniz Üniversitesi İİBF Dergisi* (7), 2007, pp.86–121.

Ulus, 8, September, 1946

Ulus, 9, September, 1946

Ulus, 10, September, 1946

Uran, Hilmi: *Hatıralarım*. Ankara, 1959.

Assist. Prof. Dr. Oktay KIZILKAYA

VIII The Causality Relationship Between Current Account Deficit and Currency Crisis: The Case of Turkey[1]

Abstract: As it is known, economic crises leave marks that affect deeply the economies of countries both during and after the crisis. Therefore, many academics and researchers try to explain the causes of economic crises. In this sense, the first crisis was to classify the crises. Economic crises are basically divided into real and financial crisis. The financial crisis, the most frequently encountered crisis in the global economic system, is the most common. In financial crises, the currency crisis is expressed as the result of the speculative attack against the national currency either as a result of the sudden depreciation of the money or as a result of the serious reductions in the international reserve level or by the coexistence of both situations. In this study, one of the hotly debated issues in recent years in Turkey, the current account deficit and its relationship with currency crisis, is analysed in the context of causality analysis using quarterly data from 1998 to 2017. Current account deficit series is calculated by current account deficit/GDP (cad), and the exchange market pressure index (EMP) is used to represent the currency crisis series. In this context, the stationarity of series is analysed by Augmented Dickey–Fuller (ADF) unit root test. In the second stage, the causality relationship between the series is investigated by the Granger causality test and the bootstrap causality test proposed by Hacker and Hatemi-J (2012). The findings conclude that the causality relationship is from the currency crisis to the current account deficit in Turkey. What is more, the causality relation could not be obtained from current account deficit to currency crisis.

Keywords: Currency Crises, Current Account Deficit, Unit Root Test, Granger Causality Test, Bootstrap Causality Test

Introduction

There have been developed several theories about the reasons for crises. Dynamics of macroeconomic and financial variables are analyzed within the frame of crises in literature. Although some of the factors that affect crises were enlightened in the literature, determining the deeper reasons for crises is still a problem.

1 This study is derived the doctoral thesis named as “The Logit-Probit Models and Neural Networks in Estimation of the Currency Crises: The Case of Turkey”. Related thesis was presented by Assistant Professor Oktay Kızılkaya in 26.05.2017.

Although there is observed main factors such as macroeconomic imbalances, internal or external shocks, there are still several questions about certain reasons for the crises. Financial crises occur in different manners in spite of they have common factors. Empirical studies expressed various stages of financial crises from small-scale financial failures to large-scale regional, national and even global crises. Financial crises generally occur before asset and credit booms and may turn into collapse in the end. Many theories that focus on the source of crises have emphasized the importance of the booms in assets and credit markets (Claessens, Kose, Laeven, & Valencia 2014, pp. 3-5-6).

Financial crises can be defined as the serious economic problems arising from the excessive increase nonperforming loans in the banking system and also the severe price fluctuations (Kibritçioğlu 2001, p. 2). There are different classifications on the types of financial crises. The International Monetary Fund (IMF) groups the crises as the currency crises, banking crises, systematic financial crises and external debt crises (IMF 1998, pp. 74–75). Reinhart and Rogoff (2009) divided crises into two different groups. While the first group includes currency and sudden stop crises, debt and banking crises are in the second group. Kibritçioğlu (2001) classified financial crises under three titles as the banking crisis, currency crisis and stock market crisis.

With reference to the expressions of Goldstein, Kaminsky and Reinhart (2000), much as there are quite a few common points in leading indicators that have the best performance in the banking and currency crises, there is still a difference to separately evaluate them. If a speculative attack on exchange value on a value causes money to lose in value or significant decreases in foreign exchange reserves or huge increases in interests, this situation can be called a currency crisis. Again, if there occurs a banking crisis at least two years before or two years later at most from the beginning of the crisis, this situation is called the twin crisis. Weaknesses in financial structure, incorrect macroeconomic policies, exchange rate system and mistakes in exchange rate fixing, problems on audit and regulation, macroeconomic conditions can be shown as the reasons for financial crises. Following items can be aligned as the macroeconomic effects of a crisis in financial markets: crunch in credit volume; increase in interests; increase in emission; decrease in production, employment, savings and investments and recession in expense and demand (Ural 2003, p. 15).

Turkish economy experienced several crises with different duration and severity before the 1980s. The Turkish economy has opened to foreign countries within the scope of the export-oriented development model; faced shocks that are out of its intervention. There occurred increases in the number and severity of the crises. Turkey that has become a chronic inflation country in the related period more frequently faced crises by adding political instability after the 1990s (Işık, Alagöz & Yıldırım 2006, p. 240; Doğru 2015, pp. 62–63). There occurred different crises from the 1990s till today such as 1994 Crisis, 2000–2001 Crisis and 2008 Global Economic Crisis. Exchange rate policy (low exchange rate policy) that excessively value TL and the financing public deficits by high-interest loan have great effects on the 1994 crisis in Turkey. A significantly short-date fund inflow was performed for Turkey in a related period; however, there occurred a crisis environment after those funds abandoned Turkey. TL was devaluated by economic stability program decisions on 5 April against 1994 crisis; an austerity package including decreasing public expenditures and increasing taxes has carried into effect. All these issues caused a long-dated recession and company bankruptcies (Seyidoğlu & Yıldız 2006, p. 10). Precautions that are taken to recover the damages of the 1994 crisis could not be completely efficient; there can be talked about a failure about eliminating the factors that create the crisis. Namely, the precautions that could not be taken after the 1994 crisis caused the 2000 and 2001 crisis (Yüksel 2016, p. 94). The underlying cause of 2000 and 2001 crises is the insecurity environment in national and foreign as the result of delaying structural reforms. Period of 2001 crisis is the deepest economic crisis period of the history of the republic; the national economy experienced the biggest depression after the downsizing in the Second World War. The greatest credit booms is at the bottom of the crisis which arose in September and spread into the whole world in 2008 in the US. Finance sector of Turkey had a less fragility problem in the 2008 global crisis in comparison with crises arose in other developing countries and both the 1994 crisis and 2000–2001 crises.

Current account deficit has become one of the biggest problems of the Turkish economy of late years. There have been conducted several studies on this issue by gaining currency of discussions about the current deficit. Reducing or at least sustainability the current account deficit is essential for sustainable economic growth and social wealth increase. Many countries experienced great changes in the current account balance by the effect of shocks in the oil prices in the second part of the 1970s. Those developments created a huge concern among policymakers and analysts; studies about determinants of current deficit have gained prominence. Sachs, Cooper and Fischer (1981) pointed out that there is no reason for worrying about them as long as high current accounts deficit creates new investment opportunities (Edwards 2002, p. 24). Studies about whether current deficit can be accepted as a signal of a crisis have increased as from the 1990s. There is not a consensus on this issue as well as some of the authors think that national economies in which high current deficit is seen become more open to the crises (Saçık & Alagöz 2010, p. 113). For other investigators, current accounts do have not a great effect on crises. With reference to literature, the ratio of current account deficit to GDP needs to be 4 %–6 % and the related value is the threshold. This study aimed to test the causality relationship between the current deficit and currency crises. The currency crisis is theoretically analyzed in the second chapter of the study. Studies on currency crises that were conducted in Turkey can be seen in the third chapter. The fourth chapter includes econometric methods and findings. There are results in the final part.

Currency Crises

With reference to Kaminsky and Reinhart (1999) with Kaminsky, Lizondo and Reinhart (1998), the currency crisis is defined as resulting the speculative attack against the national currency in sudden currency depreciation or serious decreases in international reserve level or in both two of them at the same time (Çeviş 2005, p. 9). The money of crisis country considerably loses in value during a currency crisis. Expectations relating to national currency depreciation are effective in this process and also the speculators who think that national currency will lose value continuously buy foreign currency from the market during this process. The Central Bank circles the wagons by selling foreign currency to the market to avoid related depreciation and then losses a significant part of its international reserves. Since the Central Bank cannot stand to lose its reserves more, it needs to intervene in the market by using other instruments except for selling foreign currency. The Central Bank starts to increase the interest rates under the circumstances. National currency with increasing interest rate gain prominence for the investors; thus, they avoid the national currency depreciation (Yüksel 2016, pp. 13–14).

Models that are utilized to explain the currency crises are grouped as the first generation crisis models, the second generation crisis models and the third generation crisis models. The first generation crisis models were raised to clarify the crises in Latin countries in the 1970s and 1980s. For the first generation crisis models, the key reason for the crises is the inconsistency between macroeconomic policies and the exchange rate goals of the government. Related crisis models remained incapable to explain the 1992 Europe currency crisis. For the second generation crisis models, crisis arises as the result of self-feeding expectations. 1997 Asian crisis was waxier than other crises and its spillover effects were different from other crisis models; these issues are the reasons for the third generation crisis models to take part in the economics literature. The third generation models emphasized the importance of banking and finance sector after the Asian crisis and these related models are based on the thought that banking crises and currency crises create a vicious cycle that feeds each other. These crisis models endeavor to contagion mechanisms of crisis between the countries (Altunöz 2013, p. 55; Sevim 2012, p. 24).

Literature

Many economists adopt estimation methods of crises as the work item because of reducing the effects of crises on the economy. It is seen when the literature about currency crises is analyzed that the number of studies about crisis estimation and early warning systems has increased day by day. Frankel and Rose (1996) scrutinized currency collapse for 100 developing countries by using the annual data of 1971–1992 periods. A probit model was used as the econometric method. There is not found a strong and significant relationship between current accounts deficit and the financial crises.

Milesi-Ferretti and Razin (2000) reviewed the relationship between current accounts reversals and indicators of the currency crises in the sample that consists of 105 low-income and middle-income countries in the period of 1970–1996. For their research findings, the majority of reversals does not actualize before a currency crisis or accompany a currency crisis.

Cerra and Saxena (2002) conducted a study by using an error correction model as the econometric method for the 1991 crisis in India. They concluded that current accounts deficit has a crucial role in a crisis.

Edwards (2002) aimed to review the role of current accounts on the financial crises in more than 120 developing economies over twenty-five years. He used probit model as the econometric method. For research results, every big deficit does not cause a crisis; however, big deficits should be a source of concern.

Peltonen (2006) used monthly observations of 1980–2001 period for 24 developing countries. Probit model and artificial neural networks were utilized as the method. It is concluded that current deficit/GDP variable is one of the factors that increase the crisis possibility.

About the literature about currency crises in Turkey, Ucer, Rijckeghem & Yolalan (1998) used KLR model for the 1989–1997 period. For the research results; export/import, short-dated advanced loans to exchequer/GDP, short-term external debt/GDP, real M1 and reserves/M2Y+debt stock are the most significant variables to foresee 1994 currency crisis.

Gerni, Emsen & Değer (2005) used the Linear Probability Model (LPM) and Logit Model as the econometric methods in research in which monthly data of the 1990–2004 period were utilized. It is observed at the end of the research that increasing in value of the national currency; falling industrial production index; decreasing the reserves; decreasing the ratio of public revenues to public expenditures and increasing inflation difference and interest rate differences statistically cause the crisis.

Kaya and Yılmaz (2006) used KLR Model to estimate the currency crises in Turkey by using the 1990–2002 period. For the results, the public sector borrowing requirement/GDP variable from 29 indicators is the most successful leading indicator.

Altıntaş and Öz (2007) aimed to estimate 1994 and 2001 currency crises in Turkey by the KLR model in their research in which three-month data of 1990–2005 period were used. Following items were obtained as leading indicators in order of priorities; industrial production index, capital outflow, M2/reserves, GNP, output growth, M1, IMKB (Istanbul Stock Exchange)100 index, 3-months deposit rate, and real effective exchange rate.

Karakayalı and Sayın (2010) used KLR model to estimate the 2008 crisis in Turkey by the data of the 2002–2009 period. With reference to the conclusions, industrial production index and domestic credit volume are the indicators which have the best performance.

Aktaş and Şen (2013) used Trend Analysis Method as the econometric method in their research in which annual data of the 2005–2011 period were utilized. Leading indicators were estimated to forecast the 2008 crisis in Turkey, US, UK, Greece and Italy. It is concluded in an analysis that total investments/GNP, unemployment rate, increase in merchandise and service export, total external debt (public+private)/ GNP and annual inflation rate can be used as the leading indicators.

Econometric Method and Findings

This study aimed to test the causality relationship between the current account deficit and currency crises by using quarterly data of 1998Q1–2017Q2 period. Current account deficit series is computed as current account deficit/GDP (*cad*). Exchange Market Pressure (*emp*) was used to represent the currency crises. *emp* is calculated as follows (Equation 1):

$$emp_t = \%\Delta e_t - \alpha_1 \%\Delta r_t \tag{1}$$

where, e_t shows the nominal exchange rate of the country in t time; r_t represents the reserves; α_1 shows the ratio (σ_e/σ_r) of relative change standard deviation of nominal rate ratio to the standard deviation of relative change in reserves. Data were collected from the webpage of the Central Bank of the Turkish Republic-Electronic Data Delivery System (EDDS). *cad* variable that has a seasonality effect was adjusted from seasonal effects by using the TRAMO/SEATS method.

The causality relation between current deficit and currency crises was analyzed in this study. First of all, stationarity of series was reviewed by Augmented Dickey-Fuller (ADF) unit root test. The causality relation between series was tested by Granger Causality Test and bootstrap causality test that is suggested by Hacker and Hatemi-J (2012) in the second stage.

Unit Root Test

Integration degrees of variables were analyzed by using Augmented Dickey-Fuller (ADF) unit root test. Equations (2), (3) and (4) are estimated in the ADF unit root test;

$$\Delta Y_t = \delta Y_{t-1} + \sum_{i=1}^{m} \alpha_i \Delta Y_{t-i} + u_t \tag{2}$$

$$\Delta Y_t = \beta_1 + \delta Y_{t-1} + \sum_{i=1}^{m} \alpha_i \Delta Y_{t-i} + u_t \tag{3}$$

$$\Delta Y_t = \beta_1 + \beta_2 t + \delta Y_{t-1} + \sum_{i=1}^{m} \alpha_i \Delta Y_{t-i} + u_t \tag{4}$$

The null hypothesis which expresses that the series has a unit root is $H_0{:}\delta = 0$. Tab. 1 shows the ADF test results.

As is seen in Tab. 1, ADF test results show that *emp* is stationary at level. According to ADF test, *cad* is not stationary at level; however, it becomes stationary when its first difference is computed.

Causality Analysis

It is assumed in Granger (1969) causality test that there are two variables like x and y. If the addition of the information of the variable x contributes to the prediction of the y variable, it expresses the variable x as the cause of the variable y and determines the direction of the causality from x to y. Regression equations (5) and (6) are used in the Granger causality test.

$$y_t = a_1 + \textstyle\sum_{i=1}^{p} b_{1i}\, y_{t-i} + \sum_{i=1}^{p} b_{2i}\, x_{t-i} + v_{1t} = 0 \tag{5}$$

$$x_t = c_1 + \textstyle\sum_{i=1}^{p} d_{1i}\, x_{t-i} + \sum_{i=1}^{p} d_{2i}\, y_{t-i} + v_{2t} = 0 \tag{6}$$

Tab. 1: ADF Unit Root Test Results

Variables	**ADF Test Statistics**	**Critical Values**		
		(1 %)	(5 %)	(10 %)
emp	-2.066 [6]**	-2.597	-1.945	-1.613
cad	-1.266 [0]	-2.595	-1.945	-1.614
Δ ***cad***	-8.351 [0]*	-2.595	-1.945	-1.614

Note: The values in square brackets show the optimal lag length according to AIC (Akaike Information Criteria). *, ** and *** represents significance at 1 %, 5 % and 10 %, respectively.

where, y_t and x_t show the variables in analysis; a_1 and c_1 represent the constant terms; b and d show the coefficients to be estimated; p represents the lag length; v_t is white noise.

Granger causality analysis is performed by testing whether coefficients of the lagged value of independent variable equal to zero at a certain significance level in equations (5) and (6). If b_i coefficients in equation (5) are found as different from zero at a significance level, there is a causality relationship from x to y. If d_i coefficients numbered equation (6) are different from zero at a certain significance level, there is a causality relationship from y to x. Direction of causality is defined by testing H_0 and H_1 hypotheses via Wald test if we think that Granger causality test is conducted based on regression equation (5):

$$H_o = \sum_{i=1}^{p} b_{2i} = 0 \qquad\qquad H_1 = \sum_{i=1}^{p} b_{2i} \neq 0$$

There is causality relationship from x to y in case of H_0 hypothesis is accepted. It is concluded that there is a causality relationship from y to x in case of H_1 hypothesis is accepted. Tab. 2 shows the Granger causality test results.

As is seen in Tab. 2, there is no causality relation from *cad* to *emp*. Moreover, the null hypothesis is rejected based on F-statistics that shows the causality relation from *emp* to *cad*. In other words, there can be talked about a causality relationship from currency crises to the current deficit.

Use of Granger (1969) causality tests gradually increases in empirical studies in which time series data are utilized. Stationary states of series are used in causality test of Granger (1969). Toda and Yamamoto (1995) revealed an approach that allows for a different integration degree of series. Hacker and Hatemi-J (2006) followed the procedure of Toda and Yamamoto (1995) and pointed out that the bootstrap approach gives better result in determining the critical value.

Tab. 2: Granger Causality Test Results

	F-Statistics	VAR(p)	p-value
Δ ***cad=>emp***	0.004	2	0.995
emp=>*Δ *cad	3.186**	2	0.047

Note: *, ** and *** represents significance at 1 %, 5 % and 10 %, respectively.

Toda-Yamamoto procedure is based on a lags augmentation of the VAR model. VAR (p) model is specified by Equation (7).

$$y_t = v + A_1 y_{t-1} + \cdots + A_p y_{t-p} + \varepsilon_t \quad (7)$$

In equation (7), y_t, v and ε_t are n-dimensional vectors; A_r is $n \times n$ matrix of parameters for lag r. Toda and Yamamoto (1995) suggested augmented VAR (p+d) model that can be used to test the causality between integrated variables.

$$y_t = \hat{v} + \hat{A}_1 y_{t-1} + \cdots + \hat{A}_p y_{t-p} + \cdots + \hat{A}_{p+d} y_{t-p-d} + \hat{\varepsilon}_t \quad (8)$$

where, it is assumed that order p is known; d shows the maximum order of integration of the variables. If H_0 hypothesis cannot be rejected, the kth element of y_t is not the Granger-cause the jth element of y_t (Hacker & Hatemi-J 2006, p. 1491);

H_0: the row j, column k element in A_r equals zero for r=1,…,p

Following expressions can be defined for sample size T;

$$Y := (y_1, \ldots, y_T) \text{ is } (n \times T) \text{ matrix,}$$

$$\hat{D} := (\hat{v}, \hat{A}_1, \ldots, \hat{A}_p, \ldots, \hat{A}_{p+d}) \text{ is } (n \times (1 + n(p+d))) \text{ matrix,}$$

$$Z_t := \begin{bmatrix} 1 \\ y_t \\ y_{t-1} \\ \vdots \\ y_{t-p-d+1} \end{bmatrix}, \text{is } ((1 + n(p+d)) \times 1) \text{ matrix,}$$

for $t = 1, \ldots, T$

$$Z := (Z_0, \ldots, Z_{T-1}) \text{ is } ((1 + n(p+d) \times T) \text{ matrix,}$$

$$\hat{\delta} := (\hat{\varepsilon}_1, \ldots, \hat{\varepsilon}_T) \text{ is } (n \times T) \text{ matrix.}$$

By using this notation, VAR ($p+d$) model that includes constant term ($\hat{v}$) can be written by using related notation as follows;

$$Y = \hat{D}Z + \hat{\delta} \tag{9}$$

We estimate $\hat{\delta}_U$, the ($n\times T$) matrix of estimated residuals from the unrestricted regression (9). Then the variance-covariance matrix of these residuals can be calculated as $S_U = \hat{\delta}_U'\hat{\delta}_U/T$. *vec* (column-stacking) denotes operator and $0_{n\times nd}$ denotes a zero matrix with n rows and $n(d)$ columns. Thus, $\beta=vec(v,A_1,\ldots,A_p,0_{n\times nd})$; $\hat{\beta} = vec(\hat{D})$. The Modified Wald (MWALD) test statistics that is suggested by Toda and Yamamoto (1995) can be seen in Equation (10).

$$MWALD = (C\hat{\beta})'[C((Z'Z)^{-1} \oplus S_U)\, C']^{-1}\,(C\hat{\beta}) \tag{10}$$

where, $\oplus$ is Kronecker product and C is a ($pxn(1+n(p+d)$) matrix. The null hypothesis which expressed that there is no Granger causality relation is $H_0: C\beta = 0$. MWALD test statistics is asymptotically (χ^2) distributed with the number of degrees of freedom equal to p, the number of restrictions to be tested. Hacker and Hatemi-J (2006) conducted a study to research the size properties of MWALD test and argued that test performance is low when chi-square distribution is used in small samples. Hacker and Hatemi-J (2006) offered to use bootstrap distribution to lower the size distortions. Monte Carlo simulation results of the study confirm that MWALD test that is based on bootstrap distribution has smaller size distortions in comparison with situations in which asymptotic distribution is utilized.

Lag length is determined exogenously by the estimated VAR model in Hacker and Hatemi-J (2006) procedure. Differently from Hacker and Hatemi-J (2006), the situations in which lag length is determined endogenously are researched in bootstrap causality test that is suggested by Hacker and Hatemi-J (2012).

All the causality tests in literature is based on the selected lag length; the results might be affected by the selected lag length at the same time. This is because determining the optimal lag length is a crucial issue. Various information criteria are used in literature to specify the optimal lag length. Sometimes, related information criteria may choose different lag lengths. Hatemi-J (2003, 2008) offered new information criteria that is obtained by uniting Schwarz (1978) with Hannan and Quinn (1979) information criteria to select the optimal lag length. This study determined the optimal lag length by the minimization of information criteria that is defined as below and was developed by Hatemi-J (2003, 2008).

$$HJC = \ln(det\,\hat{\Omega}_j) + j\left(\frac{n^2 lnT + 2n^2 \ln(lnT)}{2T}\right), \qquad (11)$$

$$j = 0,1, \dots, p$$

where, $det\,\hat{\Omega}_j$ shows the determinant of the estimated maximum likelihood variance-covariance matrix of residuals in VAR (j) model. n is the number of variables; T is the sample size; lt shows the natural logarithm (Hatemi-J & Uddin 2014, p. 377). Tab. 3 shows the Hacker and Hatemi-J (2012) causality test results.

As is seen in Tab. 3, there is no causality relationship from *cad* to *emp*. Moreover, since MWALD statistical values which show causality relationship from *emp* to *cad* are bigger than the critical value that is calculated by the bootstrap method, the null hypothesis is rejected. In other words, there is a causality relationship from the currency crises to the current account deficit.

Tab. 3: Hacker and Hatemi-J (2012) Causality Test Results

	MWald Test Statistics	**p-value**	***p***	**Bootstrap Critical Values**		
				1 %	**5 %**	**10 %**
cad=>emp	0.134	0.714	1	6.655	3.974	2.794
emp=>cad	8.816*	0.003	1	7.045	4.037	2.780

Note: The optimal lag length (*p*) is determined by HJC information criteria. *, ** and *** represents significance at 1 %, 5 % and 10 %, respectively.

Conclusion

In this study, one of the debated issues in recent years in Turkey, the current account deficit and its relationship with currency crisis, is analyzed in the context of causality analysis. The data used in this study are the quarterly observations from 1998Q1 to 2017Q2. First of all, stationarity of series is investigated by Augmented Dickey-Fuller (ADF) unit root test. With reference to ADF test results, the *emp* variable that represents the currency crises is stationary; the current account deficit (*cad*) is not stationary at level; however, it becomes stationary when its first difference is computed. The causality relationship between series is tested by Granger (1969) Causality Test and bootstrap causality test proposed by Hacker and Hatemi-J (2012). According to causality test results, there is a causality relationship from currency crises to the current account deficit in Turkey. However, there is no causality relationship from the current account deficit to the currency crises. Granger causality test results and Hacker and Hatemi-J (2012) bootstrap test results confirm each other. These results prove that the current deficit cannot be evaluated as a leading indicator to estimate the currency crises for Turkey.

References

Aktaş, Metin and Şen, Bünyamin: "2008 Global Ekonomik Krizinin Öncü Göstergeleri ve Ülkeler Üzerinde Bir Uygulama". *Ömer Halisdemir Üniversitesi İktisadi ve İdari Bilimler Fakültesi Dergisi* 1 (6), 2013, p. 137.

Altıntaş, Halil and Öz Bülent: "Para Krizlerinin Sinyal Yaklaşımı İle Öngörülebilirliği: Türkiye Uygulaması". *Anadolu University Journal of Social Sciences* 7 (2), 2007, pp. 19–44.

Altunöz, Utku: *Finansal Krizler, Erken Uyarı Sistemleri ve 2008 Krizi için TR-ABD Örneği*. İstanbul: Beta Basım, 2013.

Cerra, Valerie and Saxena, Sweta Chaman: "What Caused the 1991 Currency Crisis in India?". *IMF Staff Papers* 49 (3), 2002, pp. 395–425.

Çeviş, İsmail: *Para Krizlerine Ampirik Bir Yaklaşım*. Sermaye İstanbul: Piyasası Kurulu, 2005.

Claessens, Stijn, Kose, M. Ayhan, Laeven, Luc and Valencia, Fabian: *Financial Crises: Causes, Consequences, and Policy Responses*. International Monetary Fund, 2014.

Doğru, Bülent: *Türkiye'nin Yakın Dönem Ekonomik Krizleri: 1994, 2001, 2008,?*. İstanbul: Hiperlink Yayınları, 2015.

Edwards, Sebastian: *Does the Current Account Matter?. In Preventing Currency Crises in Emerging Markets*. Chicago: University of Chicago Press, 2002, pp. 21–76.

Frankel, Jeffrey A. and Rose, Andrew K.: "Currency Crashes in Emerging Markets: An Empirical Treatment". *Journal of International Economics* 41(3–4), 1996, pp. 351–366.

Gerni, Cevat, Emsen, Ö. Selçuk and Değer, M. Kemal: "Erken Uyarı Sistemleri Yoluyla Türkiye'deki Ekonomik Krizlerin Analizi". *Ekonometri ve İstatistik Dergisi* (2), 2005, pp. 39–62.

Goldstein, Morris, Kaminsky, L. Graciela and Reinhart, M. Carmen: *Assessing Financial Vulnerability: An Early Warning System for Emerging Markets*. Peterson Institute, 2000.

Granger, Clive WJ: "Investigating Causal Relations by Econometric Models and Cross-Spectral Methods". *Econometrica: Journal of the Econometric Society* 37 (3), 1969, pp. 424–438.

Hacker, R. Scott and Hatemi-J, Abdulnasser: "A Bootstrap Test for Causality with Endogenous Lag Length Choice: Theory and Application in Finance". *Journal of Economic Studies* 39 (2), 2012, pp. 144–160.

Hacker, R. Scott and Hatemi-J, Abdulnasser: "Tests for Causality between Integrated Variables Using Asymptotic and Bootstrap Distributions: Theory and Application". *Applied Economics* 38 (13), 2006, pp. 1489–1500.

Hannan, J. Edward and Quinn, G. Barry: "The Determination of the Order of an Autoregressive". *Journal of the Royal Statistical Society* (41), 1979, pp. 190–195.

Hatemi-J, Abdulnasser: "A New Method to Choose Optimal Lag Order in Stable and Unstable VAR Models". *Applied Economics Letters* 10 (3), 2003, pp. 135–137.

Hatemi-J, Abdulnasser: "Forecasting Properties of a New Method to Determine Optimal Lag Order in Stable and Unstable VAR Models". *Applied Economics Letters* 15 (4), 2008, pp. 239–243.

Hatemi-J, Abdulnasser and Uddin, Gazi Salah: "On the Casual Nexus of Remittances and Poverty Reduction in Bangladesh". *Applied Economics* 46 (4), 2014, pp. 374–382.

IMF: "Financial Crises: Characteristics and Indicators of Vulnerability in Financial Crises: Causes and Indicators". *World Economic and Financial Survey World Economic Outlook*, 1998.

Işık, Nihat, Alagöz Mehmet and Yıldırım Metin: "1990 Sonrası Türkiye'de Yaşanan Krizler: 1994, 2000 ve 2001 Krizleri". *Ekonomik Kriz Öncesi Erken Uyarı Sistemleri: Makale Derlemesi*, 2006, pp. 237–262.

Kaminsky, L. Graciela and Reinhart M. Carmen: "The Twin Crises: The Causes of Banking and Balance-of-Payments Problems". *American Economic Review* 89 (3), 1999, pp. 473–500.

Kaminsky, L. Graciela, Lizondo, Saul and Reinhart M. Carmen: "Leading Indicators of Currency Crises". *Staff Papers* 45(1), 1998, pp. 1–48.

Karakayalı, Hüseyin and Sayın Ferhan: "Öncü Göstergeler Yaklaşımıyla Türkiye'de 2008 Krizinin Değerlendirilmesi". *Finans Politik & Ekonomik Yorumlar* 47 (546), 2010, pp. 33–55.

Kaya, Vedat and Yılmaz Ömer: "Para Krizleri Öngörüsünde Sinyal Yaklaşımı: Türkiye Örneği". *Ankara Üniversitesi SBF Dergisi* 61 (2), 2006, pp. 129–155.

Kibritçioğlu, Aykut: "Türkiye'de Ekonomik Krizler ve Hükümetler, 1969–2001". *Yeni Türkiye Dergisi* 1(7), 41, 2001, pp. 174–182.

Milesi-Ferretti, Gian Maria and Razin, Assaf: "Current Account Reversals and Currency Crises: Empirical Regularities". In: *Currency Crises*. Chicago: University of Chicago Press, 2000, pp. 285–323.

Reinhart, Carmen M. and Rogoff, S. Kenneth: *This Time Is Different: Eight Centuries of Financial Folly*. Princeton, New Jersey: Princeton University Press, 2009.

Sachs, D. Jeffrey, Cooper, N. Richard, and Fischer, Stanley: "The Current Account and Macroeconomic Adjustment in the 1970s". *Brookings Papers on Economic Activity* (1), 1981, pp. 201–282.

Saçık, Sinem Yapar and Alagöz, Mehmet: "Türkiye'de Cari İşlemler Açığı Sorunu vee Borçlanma ile İlişkisi". *Ekonomi Bilimleri Dergisi* 2 (2), 2010, pp. 113–120.

Schwarz, Gideon: "Estimating the Dimension of a Model". *The Annals of Statistics* 6 (2), 1978, pp. 1–464.

Sevim, Cüneyt: *Öncü Göstergeler Yaklaşımına Göre Finansal Krizler ve Türkiye Örneği*. İstanbul: BDDK Kitapları, 2012.

Seyidoğlu Halil and Yıldız Rıfat: *Ekonomik Kriz Öncesi Erken Uyarı Sistemleri Makale Derlemesi*. İstanbul: Arıkan Basım Yayım Dağıtım, 2006.

Toda, Hiro Y. and Yamamoto, Taku: "Statistical Inference in Vector Autoregressions with Possibly Integrated Processes". *Journal of Econometrics* 66 (1), 1995, pp. 225–250.

Ucer, Murat, Rijckeghem Caroline Van and Yolalan Reha: "Leading Indicators of Currency Crises: A Brief Literature Survey and an Application to Turkey". *Yapi Kredi Economic Review* 9 (2), 1998, pp. 3–23.

Ural, Mert: "Finansal Krizler ve Türkiye". *Dokuz Eylül Üniversitesi İktisadi ve İdari Bilimler Fakültesi Dergisi* 18 (1), 2003.

Yüksel, Serhat: *Bankacılık Krizlerinin Erken Uyarı Sinyalleri: Türkiye Üzerine Bir Uygulama*. Ankara: Akademisyen Kitabevi, 2016.

Assist. Prof. Dr. İlknur BİLGEN

IX Marketing Communication During Crisis Process

Abstract: Crisis, even it is financial or not, is always an important risk for organizations. When there is a conflict between people in an organization, there is crisis too. And the best way to solve the problem is communicating. However, in this chapter, economic crises are considered. At the first part of this chapter, a general brief about crisis is given. After that, marketing communication strategies are considered. Marketing communication, which is evolved to integrated marketing communication today, seems to be unnecessary for organizations sometimes while it necessitates huge budgets. However, organizations must know that marketing communication activities' returns of investment ranges are as high as its costs.

Keywords: Crisis, Communication, Marketing Communication, Crisis Communication

Introduction

It has become vital for the enterprises to manage the importance of the right communication, which has been increasing day by day with the developing economic and social trends, at a respectable level. Although communication-perspective approaches have an increasing importance in all areas, it is seen that enterprises have to detail their activities by focusing on communication in crisis processes. Communication is not easy to achieve but has come to the forefront as critical processes to be followed. As crisis periods are one of the sine qua non for companies, it is often stated that the crisis is coming.

Economic crises affect organizations', countries' and the world's trade activities. In crisis times, organizations generally tend to minimize the costs, especially marketing costs. However, marketing communication can be the best way to get over the process.

Concept of Crisis

From the 1990s onwards, the importance of crisis management has been increasing worldwide. Crisis management, disease improvement and organizational continuity have entered into the area of interest and competence of managers in the private sector as well as the public sector. Individuals and institutions in society face uncertainties and various risks. The smallest uncertainty and risk that is ignored by being considered insignificant may be the beginning of great negativities for the enterprise, employees, society and even the country. For this reason, all enterprises, whether large or small, are required to analyze and take measures to mitigate any risks they may encounter as of their establishment (Murat and Mısırlı 2005, p.2).

Various macroeconomic negativities such as the decline in demand in economic structure, decreasing investments, increasing unemployment and ultimately decreasing the level of welfare in the crisis period are evident. In other words, the economic crisis can be defined as a periodic decline in the production of goods and services, as a result of the periodic repetitions or stagnations and the resulting mass unemployment, the decline of wages and the decline in the standard of living of people (Afşar 2011, p.144).

According to the generally accepted approach, the financial crises, which are commonly seen in the emerging markets, are mainly outlined as follows:

Money crises, banking crises, foreign debt crises and systemic financial crises. Since these crises usually follow each other, they cannot be distinguished by certain lines (Turgut 2006–2007, p.36).

There are six stages of crisis defined in the literature. They are (Arslan 2009, p.181):

a) The conceptual starting point of the crisis is characterized by the accepted cultural beliefs and norms expressed in the past approaches.
b) Incubation period is the accumulation of incidents that will lead to crisis.
c) The moment of determination is the moment when the crisis gets the attention of the decision makers and becomes perceived. If the signals are caught in time, the crisis plans are introduced and the course of the crisis is followed.
d) In the offense phase, the crisis becomes understandable by the members of institution and cannot be prevented.
e) In the recovery phase, the most important features of the crisis are revealed and tried to be controlled.
f) In the restructuring phase, institutions try to be stabilized again, and the previously accepted rules and beliefs are reviewed and the institutions are prepared for the new crises.

Corporate reputation is one of the most important key elements in crisis. Main priority in crisis process is building trust. Employees, suppliers, customers and shareholders/investors, especially companies, in the face of the crisis in the short term, not long-term strategies, they can be successful if they manage. Companies experiencing a crisis or surviving crisis have understood that reputation does not have a relationship with perceptions measured once a year. This is a continuous process and must be actively managed for 24 hours (Bilmez 2011, p.181).

Advantages of Crisis

It is stated that the crisis does not always have negative effects on the enterprises and often provides significant opportunities and can be beneficial. The most important ones are opening new markets, producing new products, executing small or large structural and cultural changes in their own businesses by operating or showing the reasons for emerging crises, disabling some strong groups and putting significant cost savings in a fast and easy way. Another advantage of the crises is that managers gain knowledge and experience from the crises. This issue is one of the important issues in the crisis management literature. In particular, what enterprises learn from the crises, how they spread this organizational learning in different levels in the enterprise and how they take measures against new crises based on this learning are important. It is argued that it is an important skill for the firms to be able to manage the crisis and to take lessons from crises and it can be an important factor in creating competitiveness in the long term (Okumuş 2003, p.209).

Crisis Management Process

Organizations can act to crisis proactive and reactive. If they have a forecast about this situation, they will probably act proactive to prevent the crisis. However, sometimes this doesn't work because of the environmental factors.

A crisis management process comprises six stages as given below (Zincir and Yazıcı 2013, p.69):

First stage – Avoiding the crisis:

Best way to prevent a potential crisis is to take precaution. It is possible to avoid some crisis by taking preventive measures.

Second stage – Preparing to manage the crisis:

When a crisis prevention activity does not work, crisis preparatory activities must be put in place. Preparatory activities are of great importance. In the process of crisis management, each person in charge of preparation should see the inevitability of the crisis in the same way as the inevitability of a death or tax and plan for it. It is not about whether the person or persons concerned is afraid of the crisis or that the organization will be weak in such situations. On the contrary, no matter how powerful the crisis situation is, it shows that the organization is aware of what is being prepared.

Third stage – Determining the crisis:

Organizations sometimes focus on the technical view and ignore the perception. However, the main cause of the crisis is the perception of society by the crisis and the perception can become a reality after a while. Therefore, if it is easy to deny the crisis, accepting its existence can be so challenging.

Fourth stage – Frosting the crisis:

When faced with a crisis situation, difficult decisions must be made and this should be done immediately. In today's ultra-communication world, the response of the organizations is not to stay silent, but to make a real statement about the crisis despite the internal disagreements. Thus, it is reported that the external environment is controlled by giving the impression that the situation is dominant. This means that the necessary actions are taken to control the crisis. Fulfilling this is much easier and faster in the modern world of communication. It will be in their interest for organizations to benefit from this speed and convenience.

Fifth stage – Solving the crisis:

Once the crisis arises, it will not wait; so being fast is vital. Action should be taken to resolve the crisis. For example, when the allegations about the electromagnetic field caused by mobile phones caused brain tumor, the manufacturers immediately put independent experts into use, so that concerns could be settled and a possible crisis was prevented.

Sixth stage – Utilizing from the crisis:

Experience is the name given to everyone's mistakes. The famous Irish writer Oscar Wilde's experience reflects every aspect of experience, and can be used in the process of benefiting from the crisis. There are some lessons to be learned in every crisis situation. Even if an organization did not succeed in the previous stages, it should be more careful if it wants to manage the crises it will face.

Marketing Communication in Crisis

Economic crisis environments are the environments where enterprises face the risk of experiencing loss of customers. Therefore, marketing strategies and actions need to be scrutinized. It can be said that the reactions of the marketing actions such as narrowing the lines, offering cheaper products, price cuts, increasing promotions and reducing intermediaries will be effective in the crisis (Özdemir and Kılıç 2011, p.46).

Communication process is presented in the figure below:

According to Fig. 1; the message is sent from a source and it goes to receiver. However, the message is not open, source encodes the message and receiver

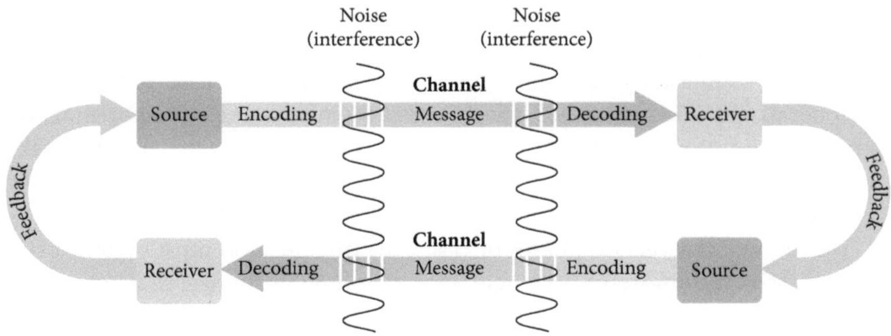

Fig. 1: Communication Process. Source: thebusinesscommunication.com 14.05.2019

decodes it. There is also a reverse proceed in this channel in which feedback is given.

In order to abolish the communication barriers that can cause crisis in this process (Elgünler and Fener 2011, p.38):

- The source should use messages able to be perceived correct,
- Messages sent by the source should not only be verbal, but also in the forms of symbols, pictures, etc.,
- Messages sent by the source should be shaped to attract the buyer's attention,
- The message must be sent with a channel that will affect the recipient,
- Communication environment should be made available for communication and
- The message should be checked with the feedback that is not understood.

Crises create a demand for knowledge. The term knowledge is used to denote the analysis of information. Managers utilize communication to collect and process information into knowledge. Crisis managers try to achieve what is often called situational awareness. Situational awareness is when managers feel they have enough knowledge to make decisions. Communication provides the knowledge to the crisis team to make decisions. By understanding the crisis situation the crisis team can make decisions about what actions to take and what messages to communicate as the crisis response. Decisions then must be communicated to the requisite stakeholders (Coombs 2009 pp. 99–100).

An effective crisis management depends on the communication. From this standpoint, communication activities during a crisis are seen as playing a dual role by helping the crisis management and caring for the image of the organization.

Groups concerned directly with the organization like board members, business partners, shareholders, customers, employees and their relatives are the first to be affected from a crisis and therefore should be informed first. Furthermore, peripheral institutions like the finance sector, the media, the governmental and political institutions, the local communities and civil initiatives too may take their consequences from the crisis and should therefore be expected to apply pressure for information demand (Akdağ and Taşdemir 2006, p.141).

Throughout the various phases of crisis, the organization must organize and act to protect its long-term corporate interest and public image; therefore, open and accurate communication is critical to the control of a crisis. Crisis communication is "the enactment of control (at least in its appearance) in the face of high uncertainty in an effort to win external audiences' confidence, in ways that are ethical. In addition to resolving the crisis and returning to normal operations, crisis management seeks to maintain or restore an organization's image, the public perception of the organization (Ray 1999, p.20).

Crisis communication is based on the issues below (Falkheimer and Heide 2010, p.512):

- Organizations are irrational and flexible.
- Communication is not a linear transmission process but rather an active and critical process of interpretation.
- Society is late modern or, in other words, increasingly heterogeneous, multicultural, fluid and changeable.

Crisis communication studies have focused on analyzing message coding strategies for different crisis situations. In analyzing the crises, it should be decided which message coding strategy should be followed after target groups are identified. It is not possible to talk about a single way or method in dealing with crises. There are strategies of development, communication, crisis, institution, defense-based, accepting, renewing and reciprocal relational messages. The message coding strategy that forms the basis of the study is Benoit's Image Correction Theory and is based on the fact that image is essential for institutions and individuals. In this theory of denial, it is a strategy used when it simply chooses to deny activities or activities that are accused. Benoit stated two subheadings for denial: simple denial and changing the offender. In the case of simple denial, if the institution is not really guilty and can determine who is guilty, the organization's name is cleared and everything may return to normal. The second strategy is avoiding responsibility, including drive, void, accidents and goodwill. If the organization expresses its activity as a result of misconduct, it may be referred to the drive. If there is a situation that arises due to lack of control over information and important factors, the invalidity may be mentioned. Accident reduces the severity of the crime related to the activity. Wrong activity is not denied, but it can be argued that this is entirely due to good intentions. Benoit's third strategy occurs when the accuser tries to reduce the degree of aggression. In this respect, Benoit has identified six sub-headings: support, reduction, differentiation, superiority, accusatory attack and compensation. Support is emphasizing the positive characteristics of the institution with its positive activities. Reduction refers to convincing that the wrong activity is not as bad as it seems. Differentiation is to distinguish the event from a less desirable but similar event. The superiority is that the unwanted event takes on a more positive content. Attacking the accuser may reduce the severity of the crime. If the accuser has little credibility, the accusation will not be taken very seriously. Compensation refers to the compensation for damages resulting from incorrect operation. The fourth strategy corrective actions that restore certain danger from criminal activity and provide specific steps to ensure that the activity will not happen again. The fifth and last image correction strategy is regret. Regret is simply an apology to accept and apologize for the action. Apologies are focused on the expectations offered by the management. This last strategy is a matter of acceptance. Instead of using a single strategy, a combination of these strategies can be used (Penpece and Madran 2015, pp.38–39).

A good crisis communication strategy should identify and prioritize when, how and which stakeholder will receive information. It should be kept in mind that information can be perceived differently in different environments such as employees, suppliers, customers, partners, society and media. For this reason, the style and announcement to be used should be determined according to the target group, but the basic messages to be transferred should always be consistent with each other. Some points to be considered in this framework are as follows (Karaağaç 2013, pp.125–126):

People's safety should always remain a top priority and should be emphasized throughout the entire communication.

Information sharing should be based solely on concrete facts and should not be predicted unless necessary.

The media should be informed of the developments in the required time and in the required manner.

Employees should be reminded of the policy of communication with the media.

The content of the institution's website should be updated as required by the event.

Even if there is no change in the current situation, the employees should be given regular and timely updated information, and the messages should be specified when the next update is made in order to manage the expectations.

In cases where a settlement needs to be evacuated, employees should be reminded of the alternate work order for the next day before leaving the workplace.

It should also be ensured that persons working remotely, posts outside the office, or those who have not come to work and contracted parties are considered when the messages are published. Complete information should be provided to employees after the crisis.

If you do not have a quick and effective crisis communication plan in place, the press will fill that 'media vacuum' with information, comment or opinion, which does more to sell their story and less to protect your business (Leighton and Shelton 2008, p.26).

An effective crisis communications plan should have the following components (Fearn-Banks 2011, p.307):

- Cover page
- Introduction
- Acknowledgements
- Rehearsal dates
- Purpose and objectives
- List of key publics
- Notifying publics
- Team identifying the crisis communications· Crisis directory
- The media spokesperson
- List of emergency personnel and local officials
- List of key media
- Spokespersons for related organizations
- Crisis communications control center
- Equipment and supplies
- Pre-gathered information
- Key messages
- Website
- Blogs and social media
- Trick questions
- List of prodromes
- List of related Internet URLs
- Evaluation form

Crisis Management in Social Media

In order to avoid falling under the avalanche, the most important steps that should be taken in the case of the crisis, which directs the attention of the media and stakeholders to the organization, is to ensure the production and flow of healthy and sustainable information. Organizations should carefully regulate the time and the coordination of those involved in crisis communication in order to effectively conduct the flow of information in the event of an unexpected, sudden developing and affecting crisis (Kavoğlu 2013, p.55).

In the literature, there is no model for crisis management in social media. However, in the light of the researches and investigations, it is seen that it is possible to deal with the crisis in social media in two ways. The first is the crises in which the real struggle is given in real life by the transfer of the crisis in the institution from the inside or outside of the institution by someone. The management of these crises in social media is possible by following the development of the crisis in a virtual environment and by small interventions. The main source of the crises transferred to social media is not clear and is of little importance in terms of attractiveness. However, it should be taken into consideration that social media may constitute the source of different crises when it is considered as the sharing point. Social media functions as an important source of news in terms of informing the target audiences and makes it necessary to work to prevent discourses that may harm the image and reputation of the institution without giving opportunity to institutions. The second kind of crisis that can be experienced in social media has started directly in this environment and it is the ongoing crises in this environment. Social media users are more interested in these types of crises because of social media. Otherwise, the dimensions of the crisis will grow and the issue in the social network of the institution will be transferred to different networks where the institution cannot directly intervene and a process will be initiated for loss of reputation (Bat and Turan Yurtseven 2014, pp. 209–210).

The second kind of crisis that can be experienced on social media started directly in this environment and it is the ongoing crises in this environment. Social media users are more interested in this type of crisis because of their social media-based interaction. Moreover, because the social media is the place where the crisis is struggled, it is necessary to have a professionally formed social media crisis plan and to act rapidly in line with this plan. In the crises that started in social media, the institution should take into account what the users have written and should respond with a gentle language in the shortest time instead of counter attack. Otherwise, the crisis will climb and the issue in the social network will be transferred to different networks that the institution cannot directly intervene and the loss of reputation that can occur cannot be prevented (Kalaycı 2017, p.334).

Conclusion

There are rules for effective communication in crisis. What is important here is to determine the reasons for the emergence of the crisis correctly. Sharing the solution models with the target audience with sincerity constitutes the cornerstone of a successful crisis communication.

You need to act quickly for an effective crisis management. The speed of information flow in crisis periods is of high importance and prevents the rumors from spreading as avalanches. The way to accomplish this is through the preplanned media relations and the well-established communication chain and the previous chapter.

The primary target group is actually employees. In this respect, the flow of accurate information to employees affects their ownership and motivation. In addition, creating trust in internal communication prevents crisis in crisis.

Being a reliable source of information affects the reputation of the institution highly. It can also be used as a surplus value if there is already a positive reputation in organizations that are aware of perception.

Probability should be estimated at the very bottom of the crisis. Suddenly the basic philosophy needed to manage or overcome a crisis that explodes is the idea that anything can happen at any moment. It is more important to identify potential risks and take precautions for the enterprises. To achieve this, a crisis management team should be established and this should be a permanent team.

Single voice is important in crisis communication. Therefore, an integrated marketing communication approach should be adopted during crisis periods and the same message should be given from all channels. Today, social media provides users with many different applications and tools. Most of the applications have specific working principles and are in different categories according to their purposes, but they can basically work as a whole and provide a full service for users. Crisis periods require effective use of social media in terms of communication.

References

Afşar, Muharrem: "Küresel Kriz ve Türk Bankacılık Sektörüne Yansımaları". *Eskişehir Osmangazi Üniversitesi İİBF Dergisi* 6(2), 2011, pp. 143–171.

Akdağ, Mustafa and Taşdemir, Erdem: "Krizden Çıkmanin Yolları: Etkin Bir Kriz İletişimi". *Selçuk İletişim* 4(2), 2006, pp. 141–157.

Arslan, Aykut: "Kriz Yönetiminde Liderlik". *Akademik Bakiş Uluslararası Hakemli Sosyal Bilimler E-Dergisi* 18, 2009, pp. 179–190.

Bat, Mikail and Turan Yurtseven, Çağla: "Sosyal Medyada Kurumsal Kriz Yönetimi: Onur Air Örneği". *Gümüşhane Üniversitesi İletişim Fakültesi Elektronik Dergisi* 2(3), 2014, pp. 197–223.

Bilmez, Esra: "Kriz Döneminde Kurumsal İtibar Yönetiminin Önemi". *Selçuk Üniversitesi Sosyal Bilimler MYO Dergisi* 14(1–2), 2011, pp. 173–188.

Coombs, W. Timothy: *Conceptualizing Crisis Communication in* Heath, Robert L. and O'Hair, H. Dan (Ed.): *Handbook of Risk and Crisis Communication*. New York: Routledge, 2009.

Elgünler, Tuğçe Çedikçi and Fener, Tuğba Çedikçi: "İletişimin Kalitesini Etkileyen Engeller ve bu Engellerin Giderilmesi". *The Turkish Online Journal of Design, Art and Communication* 1 (1), 2011, pp. 35–39.

Falkheimer, Jesper and Heide, Mats: *Crisis Communicators in Change: From Plans to Improvisations* in Coombs, W.Timothy and Holladay, Sherry J. (Ed.): *The Handbook of Crisis Communication*. London: Wiley-Blackwell, 2010.

Fearn-Banks, Kathleen: *Crisis Communications: A Handbook Approach*. New York: Routledge. 2011.

Kalaycı, Beyza Nur: "Sosyal Medyada Kriz İletişimi; Turkcell Örneği". *1. Uluslararası İletişimde Yeni Yönelimler Konferansı*. İstanbul, 2017, pp. 331–341.

Karaağaç, Tonguç: "Kriz Yönetimi ve İletişim". *İstanbul Üniversitesi Siyasal Bilgiler Fakültesi Dergisi* 49, 2013, pp. 117–132.

Kavoğlu, Samet: "Güncel Bir Olgu Olarak Yeni Medya Ve Kriz İletişimi: Örnek Vaka Analizi". *Gümüşhane Üniversitesi İletişim Fakültesi Elektronik Dergisi* 2(1), 2013, pp. 49–63.

Leighton, Nick and Shelton, Tony: *Proactive Crisis Communication Planning* in Anthonissen, Peter F. (Ed.): *Crisis Communication: Practical PR Strategies for Reputation Management and Company Survival*. London: Kogan Page, 2008.

Murat, Güven and Mısırlı, Kamuran: "Küçük ve Orta Ölçekli İşletmelerde Kriz Yönetimi: Çaycuma Örneği". *ZKÜ Sosyal Bilimler Dergisi* 1(1), 2005, pp. 1–19.

Okumuş, Fevzi: "Işletmelerde Kriz Yönetimi ve Krizlerin İşletmeler Üzerine Olası Etkileri". *Atatürk Üniversitesi İktisadi ve İdari Bilimler Dergisi* 17(1–2): 2003, pp. 203–212.

Özdemir, Erkan and Kılıç, Serkan: "2008 Küresel Ekonomik Krizi ve İnşaat Sektörü: Pazarlama Açısından Bir Alan Araştırması". *Anadolu Üniversitesi Sosyal Bilimler Dergisi* 11(2), 2011, pp. 43–68.

Penpece, Dilek and Madran, Canan: "Üniversitelerde Kriz İletişimi". *Marmara Üniversitesi Öneri Dergisi* 11(44), 2015, pp. 33–60.

Ray, Sally J.: *Strategic Communication in Crisis Management: Lessons from the Airline Industry*. New York: Quorum Books. 1999.

Turgut, Ahmet: "Türleri, Nedenleri ve Göstergeleriyle Finansal Krizler". *TÜHİS İş Hukuku ve İktisat Dergisi* 20(4–5): 2006, pp. 35–46.

Zincir, Oya and Yazıcı, Selim: "Kriz Yönetimi ve Afetlerde Sosyal Medya Kullanımı". *İstanbul Üniversitesi Siyasal Bilgiler Fakültesi Dergisi* 49, 2013, pp. 65–82.

Research Assistant Ismail Ercan BORU

X The Effects of the Global Crisis on Turkish Banking Sector[1]

Abstract: Thanks to communication technologies we can eliminate the boundaries among countries and also making their economies dependable to each other. The global financial crisis has negatively affected both developed and developing countries. The housing bubble in the US has triggered the financial crisis and it has spread out to all over the world. All financial sectors have been affected by the crisis and the global economy suffered large losses. This financial crisis has negatively affected countries in terms of currency rates, unemployment rates and industrial productions. Although many huge international banks bankrupted in developed countries, Turkish banking sector has been less affected by the global financial crisis. The main purpose of this study is to determine how Turkish banking sector has been affected limitedly compared to its peers. Main point of this study is that Turkish banking sector has successfully overcome the side effects of the global financial crisis thanks to strong financial structure after the reconstruction in 2001. Consequently it can be said that Turkish banks are ready for crisis with the measures taken before crisis and regulations in the financial markets.

Keywords: Global crisis, Banking sector, Financial markets

Introduction

Due to the globalization, there is no physical border among the countries in terms of global trade. Actually, the globalization consists of two main legs. The first one is tradable goods and services and the second one is virtual market that is composed of financial transactions. After globalization, the finance sector has been ahead of the industry.

It is possible to examine the US economy as two terms before the 2008 crisis. First, there was a period of regular growth in the US that had started in 1990 and continued until 1997. Throughout this period, inflation rate kept at low levels, unemployment rate decreased and average rates of growth were %3. However, growth rates in the US economy have slowed in 2000. After this slowdown, there have been very important developments in the US and the economy between 2004 and 2006. Between 2001 and 2006 is the second period to be examined

1 This article is derived from the master's thesis named as "the effects of the global crisis on Turkish economy"

before the global crisis. The following developments occurred in this period in terms of the world economies (Yücel and Kalyoncu 2010, pp.54–69):

- There was a tendency of inflation rates.
- There was an abundance of liquidity and decreased in interest rates in the world. Due to low interest rates, companies borrowed high amounts of money in order to grow.
- Prices in the real estate market rose excessively.

It is obvious that economic crises have negative effects of stability and economic growth. The economic crisis that arises in a country can easily affect other countries. Financial crisis that occurred in the US has affected all over the world, especially emerging markets. There are different variables which are affected by the financial crisis such as inflation, unemployment and growth rates. The main purpose of this study is the Turkish financial crisis to investigate the effects on the banking sector.

Types of Financial Crises

Crisis is the concept which is used frequently in daily life and in different fields of science. It is possible to call the situation that crisis comes to exist in unexpected or unpredictable moments, and also it creates a lot of problems in micro and macro level.

Feldstein collects financial crises under four headings:

a. Current account crises
b. Balance sheet crises
c. Money crises caused by bank-panic
d. Influence crises and irrational speculation

Financial crises can be separated as banking crises, foreign exchange crisis and stock market crisis. Banking crises may occur due to reasons such as a large amount of deposits in banks, withdrawal of banks and decline in the rate of return of loans given by banks and banks to lose a large proportion of the capital. A crisis in the banking system can take place in two stages. In the first stage, one or more banks are affected and then all of the banking system are affected by the crisis. The second stage is the crisis spread throughout the system. There is no doubt that all economic system has negatively affected increasing interest rates, credit costs and inadequacies in meeting credit demands.

According to econometric studies there was a high correlation between exchange rate collapses and banking crises. On the other hand, the probability of conversion money crises into the financial crises is very high. For example, money crises were transformed into systemic financial crises in US the early 1980s, Scandinavia in the early 1990s, Mexico in 1995 and Asia in 1997 (Kaminsky and Reinhart 1996, pp.6–7).

Economic crises are divided into two groups in terms of the formation. The first one is the "reel sector" crisis. These crises reflect their reflections as an inflation in goods and services markets crises and stagnation crises; unemployment crises in labor markets. The second group is the extreme imbalances in the financial markets, especially financial crisis which arise mainly due to problems in money markets (Yücel and Kalyoncu 2010, pp.54–69). Financial crises can create a great destructive effect on the real economy and also disrupt the effective of functioning of the markets (Taylor 2009, p.7).

Financial Crises in Historical Process

The reasons for the emergence of crises in the world are different and the measures taken differ. Looking at the history of crises in the world, the crisis in England, which is known the cradle of capitalism, is the first known economic crisis in 1845. This crisis had endured about 10 years. Secondly, the crisis in 1873 that started in the aftermath of the US civil war. The crisis started with bank sinking and stock market depression and has affected a large part of the real sector.

After the World War I, the US economy began to grow up rapidly by attracting investment especially from Europe and rest of the world. However, it caused to increase the price of security market and balloons began to seem at the financial markets. As a result of these movements, a big financial crisis occurred in the US called World Economic Depression. There are some reasons that caused the 1929 World Economic Crisis, such as imbalances between financial conditions of companies, bank structures problems in the balance of payments and insist on the gold standard system.

Another big crisis that happened in the 1970s called oil crisis started with the collapse of the Bretton Woods System. There was a large increase in oil prices because it was indexed to gold price. Oil prices increased fourfold in 1973–1974 and in 1978–1979. The increase in oil price shocks has affected the whole world, especially in less developed countries (Delice 2003, pp.57–81).

There were 2 big economic crises in 1994. The first one is Mexico crises which is known as "peso crisis" or "tequila crisis". The currency of Mexico erupted because of the sudden depreciation of Peso. Loose money and credit policies were one of the reasons for this crisis.

The second one is the Turkey economic crisis that happened in 1994. Turkish lira was devaluated because of the financial and economic uncertainty. The main factors of the 1994 crisis that caused financial stability as follows (Alpago 2002, p.35):

- The burden of the deficits of social security institutions was increasing.
- The government could not find low-interest debt so central bank used its own fund and it caused hyperinflation.
- Both public deficit and domestic debt were seen to be high in 1993.
- The cost of domestic borrowing was very high.
- The current account deficit has reached very high levels.
- Short-term capital movements were at very high levels.

Causes of Global Crisis

Financial markets have experienced an extraordinary year in 2008 which was based on the US. Many economists believe that it was the worst financial crisis since 1930s (Reuters 2009). One of the main ideas and the strongest one is that this crisis derived from the Asian economic crisis that is substantially composed of emerging markets and some developing countries such as Turkey, Argentina and Brazil faced economic distress (Diamond and Rajan 2009). These countries were very important for developed countries because they were borrowing money from abroad in order to finance their economies and major importers of capital. However, they reduced consumption, protecting themselves of foreign assets and investments were cut back by households, corporations and governments so that they became exporters of capital (Krugman, *the New York Times*).

Export-led growth was the best way to protect the country against economic and financial crises. As time goes on, developing countries have got a huge foreign exchange reserves and most of the money went to US as consumption. The low interest rates encouraged the demand for housing and house prices started to increase because of high demand (Diamond and Rajan 2009, pp. 6–7). Additionally, banks encouraged the borrowers those who want to use credit in order to buy house because they had borrowed almost the full value of the property. It provided a huge advantage for borrowers if anything goes wrong in the future because it was fully financed by banks and they can easily walk away from the mortgage (Carmassi, et al. 2009, p.990). Uygur stated that although Turkish economic growth performance and economic situation are quite sparkle between 2002 and 2007, borrowers would not use credit easily. It was mainly

Tab. 1: Mortgage Originations and Subprime Securitization. Sources: Inside Mortgage Finance, the 2007 Mortgage Market Statistical Annual, Key Data (2006), Joint Economic Committee (October 2007).

	Total Mortgage Originations (Billions)	Subprime Originations (Billions)	Subprime Share in Total Originations (%of dollar value)	Subprime Mortgage Backed Securities (Billions)	Percentage of Subprime Securitized (%of dollarvalue)
2001	$2,215	$190	8.6 %	$95	50.4 %
2002	$2,885	$231	8.0 %	$121	52.7 %
2003	$3,945	$335	8.5 %	$202	60.5 %
2004	$2,920	$540	18.5 %	$401	74.3 %
2005	$3,120	$625	20.0 %	$507	81.2 %
2006	$2,980	$600	20.1 %	$483	80.5 %

because of keeping the banks under tight control in order to prevent loan repayment problems during the credit period (Uygur 2010, pp. 45–47).

The US financial sector was very powerful and more profitable than before and also only a few investment banks and insurance companies dominated this industry. At this time, three rating agencies have evaluated them and gave information for investments (Diamond and Rajan, 2009, p.608). Thanks to easy credit conditions and low interest rates, banks borrowed huge amount of money to their customers and they did not to take any notice of borrowers' repayment capacity. Indeed, they borrowed money whoever wants even if they do not have any income, in other words it is called ninja (no income, no jobs, and no assets) (Lal 2010, p.272).

As shown in Tab. 1, it is observed that sub-threshold loans have increased between 2004 and 2006. In 2006, 20 % of total mortgage loans were given low income level citizens. More importantly, in 2006 80 % of the sub-threshold loans were sold to other financial markets through securitization.

The house prices have increased dramatically in this period not just in the US, but also in the UK, Spain and Ireland until 2006 (*The Economist* 2007). Many investors believed that increasing in the price of households is artificial and it will lead to a big problem in the real estate market sooner or later. However, Coskun (2011) argued that Turkish housing market is quite strong thanks to powerful banking sector and socio-economic structure.

Investment banks created some derivatives in order to give an opportunity to investors to invest in the US. This innovation was different from the old system. In the old system, when people borrowed money from the lender, they paid it on a regular basis and money went to the lender. Naturally, lender was very careful and considered the repayment capacity of the borrowers. However, in the new system, lenders sold these mortgages to the investment banks and then investment banks combined all loans as a derivative called CDO (collateralized debt obligation) and sold these loans to the investors (Lysandrou 2011, pp. 326–330). Such kind of derivatives was accumulating in the balance sheet of banks as a toxic asset. However, keeping toxic assets was restricted by Turkish government because it makes banking sector more vulnerable and less powerful (Bakir and Onis 2010, pp. 82–84). Thanks to this innovation, when borrowers paid their mortgages, the money went to investors all over the world. The CDOs became very popular because rating agencies evaluated the CDOs by giving AAA rating which means that it is the safest and highest investment rate. It was very important for investment banks in order to generate income because the more they sold CDOs, the higher profit they can earn (Diamond and Rajan 2009. p. 9).

Previous studies showed that the high level of leverage ratio contributed to financial crisis. The meaning of leverage ratio is that the proportion between borrowed money and a bank's or company's own money (Ghosh and Sherman 1993, p. 579). Prior to the crisis, investment banks increased their borrowing and became highly leveraged. It was mainly because of the Securities and Exchange Commission (SEC) decided to let banks to increase their level of debt. This over-leveraged made financial institutions more vulnerable, increased risk level and contributed to outbreak of crisis (Simkovic 2009, p.253).

The US five big investment banks increased dramatically their leverage between 2003 and 2007. The leverage level reached up to 33 to 1 in 2007 which means that if asset value decreases 3 %, they will be insolvent. In addition, the total amount of debt of these five investment banks is 4.1 trillion dollars in 2007 which is equal to 30 % of US nominal GDP. It is quite obvious that leverage became very frightening and began to threat financial markets (Labaton 2008).

There was another problem in the financial markets which is called credit default swaps (CDS). It is a bilateral derivative which can be used to protect against default. The world largest insurance company called AIG was selling these derivatives to investors those who want to protect themselves against default. If investor agrees to pay money for credit default swaps, they would buy it. This is like an insurance policy between seller and investor which means that if CDO goes bad, seller promises to pay all losses (Arner 2009, pp. 120–122). On the other hand, there were speculators in the market and they could also buy these swaps. Obviously, this system generated huge profits for company in a short term; therefore, they continued to use this method until it caused the bankruptcy in the long term. Basically, although this system may be seemed very

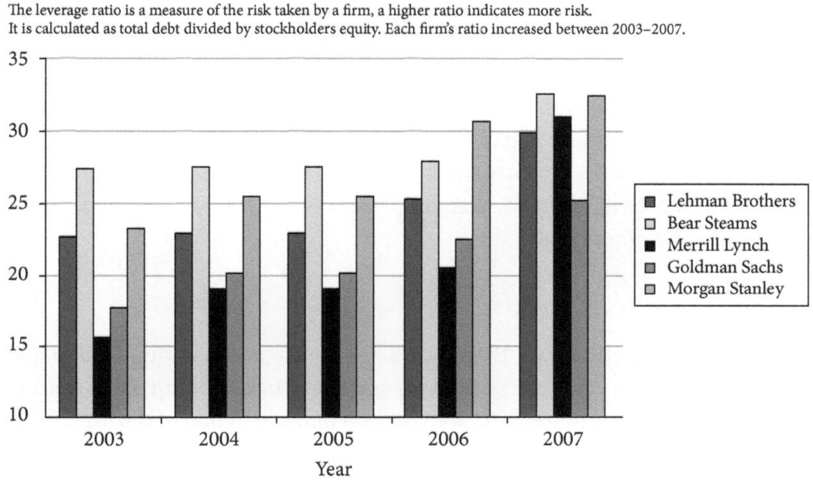

Fig. 1: Leverage Ratios for Major Investment Banks

complex, it was worked on a simple insurance transaction. However, the main difference is that they could insurance a single CDS more than one person so that if something goes bad, the number of losses would be very high in this system.

Before the 2001 crisis, there was a stabilisation programme implementing in Turkey in order to strength the economy and prompt the foreign investment. The main aim of this program is that to compete with the chronic inflation by using crawling peg exchange rate regime. The main characteristics of this program can be classified as follows (Temiz and Gokmen 2001, pp. 6–7):

- Financial sector adjustment (restructuring and reform in the sector),
- Using nominal exchange rate as the pillar,
- Far teaching indexation in the government sector,
- Managing the fiscal performance for a sweeping public sector consolidation,
- Intensified privatisation,
- Implementation of a structural reform in the social security system, government budget expenditures, agricultural sector and infrastructural investments,
- Banknote issue only in compliance with foreign exchange purchases by the Central Bank of the Republic of Turkey (CBRT) and no sterilisation by monetary policy.
- Because they knew that it was the only way to finish economic crisis (Carkoglu 2002).

The government made some financial and structural adjustments after the election, especially in banking sector because the main reason behind the 2001 crisis is that the lack of inspection and high debt ratio. In addition, the new government has faced some serious problems such as poverty alleviation and unemployment. Therefore, the government began to struggle with the poverty under the leadership of the World Bank (Bozkurt and Yalman 2011, pp. 6–8). It is important note that it was not a temporary implementation because JDP government assured these projects by making law.

Banking System in Turkey

Before the global credit crisis, there was a relatively good banking system and a strong fiscal structure in Turkey. It is argued that Turkish financial system was established on the base of banking and Turkish banks had one of the highest capital adequacy ratios in the world. Furthermore, the Central Bank of Turkey had a very high foreign reserve almost 77$ billion in September 2008. There is also important note that Turkey had concluded IMF stand-by arrangement in the middle of 2008 (Onis and Guven 2010).

Being affected by any financial turmoil or political crisis in the world is inevitable. Naturally, most of the emerging economies were affected by the recent global crisis and suffer from bad external financial conditions. The slowdown in the Turkish economy activity has started in the first half of the 2008 and it has put on a brake on the economy compared to last five years' growth performance. It was not only a special case for Turkey, but also the majority of countries have been affected by this crisis in a negative way. Marc Auboin, an economic counsellor in the World Trade Organisation, stated that "*The World Bank estimates that 85–90 % of the fall in world trade since the second half of 2008 is due to falling international demand, and 10–15 % is attributable to a fall in the supply of trade finance.*" (Uygur 2010, pp. 31–33). Although the majority of developed countries such as the US and many European countries had affected the crisis very badly, its impacts on the Turkish economy have been limited. The reasons of these limitations can be classified under 4 main headings which are healthy and powerful banking sector, strong foreign reserves, floating exchange rate regime and monetary and fiscal discipline policies (Babacan 2009).

There were not any banks transferred to the SDIF during the global crisis, whereas the number of banks to be transferred to the SDIF was eight in 2001. It clearly shows that the banking sector is very powerful and still on its feet. Furthermore, there was no reduction in the profitability and had a better balance

	1999	2002	2008	06/2009
Total Number of Banks (I + II)	81	54	45	45
I: Commercial (Deposit) Banks	62	40	32	32
(1) State	4	3	3	3
(2) Private	31	20	11	11
(3) SDIF	8	2	1	1
(4) Foreign, Founded in Turkey	5	4	11	11
(5) Foreign, Branches	14	11	6	6
II: Development and Investment Banks	19	14	13	13
(1) State	3	3	3	3
(2) Private	13	8	6	6
(3) Foreign	3	3	4	4

Tab. 2: Ownership and Number of Banks in Turkey 1999–2009 June

sheet compared to other international banks. The reason why Turkish banks have been very strong during the crisis is that they did not involve any toxic financial instruments in their balance sheet (Uygur 2010, pp. 22–25).

In addition, due to having a healthy banking system, Turkish banks found foreign credit at a lower cost compared to other emerging countries. The main reason behind this achievement is that creditor relied on the Turkish financial system and political stability. Consequently, it made the banks relatively liquid and stronger than competitors (Stokes and Rogovic 2009). Furthermore, Stokes and Rogovic argued that five factors have contributed to having a healthy banking sector which is asset quality, liquidity risks, capital adequacy, foreign exchange exposure and profitability.

As shown in the figure, Turkey has the best loans/deposits rate among selected emerging markets. Turkish loans to deposit ratio is below 100 % with Czech Republic. Turkish banks accessed to low cost of funding and almost 60 % deposits are generating of total funding. It is a huge advantage for Turkish banks to reducing credit squeeze during the crisis.

There is no doubt that joint ventures and partnership played an important role in this achievement. Before 2000, the market share of foreign banks in Turkey was less than 5 percent but thanks to banking reforms after the 2001 crisis, the total share in the sector reached almost 40 %. (Kartal 2011, p. 2018–2020). Furthermore, Macoevi (2009) stated that there are two important factors that

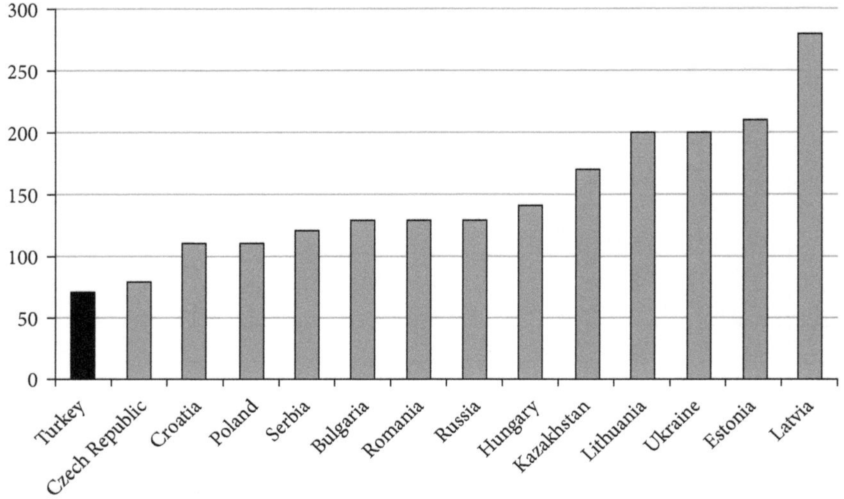

Fig. 2: Loans/Deposist (%) in Selected Emerging Markets. Source: IMF Global Financial Stability Report, April 2009

should not be forgotten in terms of soundness of Turkish banking sector which are *'successful implementation of a reform programme supported by the IMF and the opening up of accession of negotiations with the European Union'*.

Conclusion

There were some severe financial economic crises in developed and developing countries in 1990s. Although each of these crises has their own reasons but three common factors are determinative. They are macro disruption of economic balances, fragile structure of financial systems and discrepancy between domestic policies and exchange rate regime.

The world economy experienced heavy losses that began in 2007 in the US and spread to the countries of the world in 2008. The starting point of the crisis is that growing of the loan bubble of housing in the US and it was eventually bursting. Low interest rates led investors to different areas as a result of the expansionary monetary policies that has implemented in the US since the early 2000s. However, credit risk was ignored during these transactions. Due to the spread of risk to the whole world, the financial crisis in the US has turned into a major economic crisis.

All of the developed and developing countries was affected by the global crisis. Financial institutions in many countries have faced major losses and bankruptcy. Credit supply has decreased in the banking sector as a result of the crisis. The uncertainty of the crisis caused to reduce the consumption of households and firms and investment expenditures, so that this behaviour causes the demand for credit to shrink. As a result of this, a global recession has occurred.

The global crisis has also left important influences on Turkish economy. It has been observed that export figures have decreased due to reducing production and increasing unemployment. The global crisis has also affected the performance of the Turkish banking sector. In this study, it was investigated to the effects of the global crisis on Turkish banking sector.

References

Alpago, Hasan: *IMF-Türkiye İlişkileri*. İstanbul: Ötüken Yayınları, 2002.

Arner, Douglas Wayne: "The Global Credit Crisis: Causes and Consequences". *The International Lawyer* 43 (1), 2009, pp. 91–136.

Babacan, Ali: "Global Financial Crisis and the Turkish Economy". *Speech at LSE* 17, September 2009.

Bakir, Caner: "Wobbling but Still on Its Feet: The Turkish Economy in the Global Financial Crisis". *South European Society and Politics* 14 (1), March 2009, pp. 71–85.

Bakir, Caner and Onis, Ziya: *The Regulatory State and Turkish Banking Reforms in the Age of Post-Washington Consensus*. International Institute of Social Studies, 2010.

Bozkurt, Sümerjan and Yalman, Galip. L: *Case Study: AKP Governments and the Social and Labour Market Policy Transformations in Turkey in the 2000s*, retrieved 14.05.2019 from, http://www.emergingcountries.org/pdf/labour%20 market.social%20policy.Turkey.pdf

Carkoglu, Ali: "Turkey's November 2002 Elections: A New Beginning?". *Middle East Review of International Affairs (MERIA)* 6 (4), December 2002, pp. 30–41.

Carmassi, Jacopo et al: "The Global Financial Crisis: Causes and Cures". *Journal of Common Market Studies* 47 (5), 2009, pp. 977–996.

Coskun, Yener: "The Global Financial Crisis and the Turkish Housing Market: Is There a Success Story?". *Housing Finance International* 25 (3), 2011, p. 6–14.

Delice, Güven: "Finansal Krizler: Teorik ve Tarihsel Bir Perspektif". *Erciyes Üniversitesi İktisadi ve İdari Bilimler Fakültesi Dergisi* (20), Ocak-Haziran, 2003, pp. 57–81.

Diamond, Douglas. W. and Rajan, Ragruham: "The Credit Crisis: Conjectures about Causes and Remedies". *American Economic Review* 99 (2), 2009, pp. 606–610.

Feldstein, Martin: "Self-Protection for Emerging Market Economies". *NBER Working Paper Series* 6907, January 1999, pp. 1–25.

Ghosh, Dilip. K. and Sherman, G. Robert: "Leverage, Resource Allocation and Growth". *Journal of Business Finance and Accounting* 20 (4), June 1993, pp. 575–582.

Joint Economic Committee of the U.S. Congress: *The Subprime Lending Crisis*, retrieved 14.05.2019 from, https://www.streetdirectory.com/travel_guide/72774/real_estate/solutions_for_the_subprime_lending_crisis.html

Kaminsky, Graciela and Reinhart, Carmen: "The Twin Crises: The Causes of Banking and Balance of Payments Problems Board of Governors of Federal Reserve System". *International Finance Discussion Paper* (544), March 1996, pp. 1–27.

Kartal, Fikret: "The Turkish banking sector in the third after the 2008 global crisis". *African Journal of Business Management*, 6(5), 2012, pp. 2015–2025.

Krugman, Paul: *Revenge of the Glut*, retrieved 12.01.2019 from, www.nytimes.com.

Labaton, Stephen: *Agency's '04 Rule Let Banks Pile up New Debt*, retrieved 31.10 2019 from, www.nytimes.com.

Lal, Deepak: "The Great Crash of 2008: Causes and Consequences". *Cato Journal* 30 (2), Spring/Summer, 2010, pp. 265–277.

Lysandrou, Photis: "Global Inequality as One of the Root Causes of the Financial Crisis: A Suggested Explanation". *Economy and Society*, 40 (3), August 2011, pp. 323–344.

Macoevi, Mihai: "Growth and Economic Crises in Turkey: Leaving Behind the Turbulent Past". *Economic and Financial Affairs* (386), 2009, pp. 1–39.

Öniş, Ziya and Güven, Ali. Burak: "Global Crisis, National Responses: The Political Economy of Turkish Exceptionalism". *Koç University-TUSIAD Economic Research Forum Working Papers* (1013), 2010, pp. 1–23.

Simkovic, Michael: "Secret Liens and the Financial Crisis of 2008". *American Bankruptcy Law Journal* (83), 2009, pp. 253–297.

Taylor, John. B: "The Financial Crisis and the Policy Responses: An Empirical Analysis of What Went Wrong". *NBER Working paper* (14631), 2009, pp. 1–32.

Temiz, Dilek and Gokmen, Aytaç: "The Comparative Effects of 2000–2001 Financial Crises and 2008 Global Crisis on the Turkish Economy". *International Journal of Economic and Administrative Studies* 2 (4), 2010, pp. 1–24.

Uygur, Ercan: "The Global Crisis and the Turkish Economy". *Twin Global Economy Series* (21), 2010, pp. 1–74.

Fatih, Yücel and Hüseyin, Kalyoncu: "Finansal Krizlerin Öncü Göstergeleri ve Ülke Ekonomilerini Etkileme Kanalları: Türkiye Örneği". *Maliye Dergisi* (159), 2011, pp.54–69.

About Authors

Ekrem Yaşar Akçay
ekremyasarakcay@hakkari.edu.tr
Ekrem Yasar Akçay is an assistant professor at Hakkâri University, Department of Political Sciences and International Relations. He completed his master's studies at Suleyman Demirel University, Institute of Social Sciences, Department of International Relations in 2010. Then he got his PhD at Ankara University, Institute of Social Sciences, Department of International Relations. He was a researcher at Humboldt Universitat zu Berlin and Wroclaw University for six months. He has many articles that are published in numerous academic journals. His book *"Türkiye-AB İlişkileri ve İmtiyazlı Ortaklık Meselesi" (The Privileged Partnership Question in Turkey-EU Relations)* is published in February 2016 by Imaj Publishers. His other book, *"Soğuk Savaş Döneminde Avrupa: Temel Konular Üzerinden Avrupa'nın Dönüşümünü Anlamak" (Europe in the Cold War Era: Understanding the Transformation of Europe over the Issues)* is published in September 2017 by Kriter Publishing.

İdris Turan
turan.idris@gmail.com
İdris Turan was born in Afyonkarahisar, Turkey. He graduated from Computer Science Education in Gazi University in 2009. He began MA program in Sakarya University and the 2nd undergraduate program in Anadolu University (Open University) about International Relations in 2010. He graduated from MA in 2013 and from 2nd undergraduate in 2014. He began a PhD about International Relations in 2014 in Sakarya University. He is planning to graduate from PhD in 2019.

Fatma Ökde
Fatma Okde was born in Ardahan, Turkey. She graduated from Department of Political Science and Public Administration in Kirikkale University in 2010. She got her master's degree from Department of Political Science and Public Administration in Kirikkale University, in 2013. She began PhD program, Department of Political Science and Public Administration, in 2015 in Kirikkale University. She is planning to graduate from PhD in 2018.

Habip Demirhan

Habip Demirhan is an assistant professor of Public Finance at Hakkâri University. He graduated from Ankara University Faculty of Political Sciences in 2005. During 2006–2011, he worked with local governments. Shortly after that he started his academic career in Hakkâri University as a research assistant. He took his master's degree in 2013 and his PhD in 2017 in Public Finance at Dokuz Eylul University Social Sciences Institute. He has been working as an Assistant Professor in Public Finance Department at Hakkâri University since September 2017.

Burak Ökde

Burak Okde was born in Elazig, Turkey. He graduated from the Department of Business Administration in Marmara University in 2010. He got his master's degree from the fiscal economy department in Sakarya University, in 2014. He began PhD program, Department of Fiscal Economy in 2014 in Gazi University. He is planning to graduate from PhD in 2018.

Selim Demez

selimdemez@hakkari.edu.tr

Selim Demez is an assistant professor of Political Economics in the Department of Economics at Hakkari University. He was born in Malatya, Turkey, and educated in Malatya with BA and MA degrees in Economics at Inonu University. Dr. Demez holds a PhD in Economics from Istanbul University and is coauthor of *Exchange-Rate Volatility's Impact on Turkey's Exports: An Empirical Analysis for 1992–2010, Validity of Fisher Effect for Turkish Economy: Cointegration Analysis (2012), Relationship between Real Oil Price and Real Exchange Rate: The Case of Turkey (2013), Testing the Validity of Wagner's Law: 1998–2004, The Case of Turkey, Balancing Islamic and Conventional Banking for Economic Growth Empirical Evidence from Emerging Economies (2016).*

Zekai Özdemir

zekoz@istanbul.edu.tr

Zekai Özdemir is a professor in the Department of Economics at Istanbul University. He has articles on economic policy, development, monetary policy, and agricultural economics. He teaches courses in microeconomics, world economics, and regional economics at graduate and undergraduate level. He has also authored book and book chapters on microeconomics, market economics, stability policy, agricultural economics, and foreign trade.

İhsan Seddar Kaynar
Ihsan Seddar Kaynar completed his master's studies and got his PhD degree from the Economic History Department of Marmara University. He conducted research at the Centre for Economic History, University of Reading (UK). His research interests involve the transition from Ottoman Empire to the Republic of Turkey, the development of hazelnut agriculture in the Black Sea Region, Cyprus, under the British occupation and political economy of Turkey. His dissertation received the award of Koç University VEKAM Research Grant in 2015. Currently, he is teaching in Hakkari University, in the Department of Economics.

Oktay Kizilkaya
Oktay Kızılkaya is an assistant professor in Department of Economics at Hakkari University. He was born in Malatya, Turkey. He graduated with a BA degree in Maths at Fırat University and an MA degree in the Department of Econometrics at Inonu University. Dr. Kızılkaya is a PhD graduate in Department of Econometrics in Inönü University and is coauthor of *Are the Kaldor's Laws Valid? Panel Data Analysis under Cross Section Dependency for NIC Countries (2015), Testing of Relation among Manufacturing Sector, Economic Growth and Productivity in Turkey within the Framework of Kaldor Laws: An Econometric Analysis (2014), Artificial Neural Networks Models Performance Comparisons for Turkey's GDP Forecasting (2015), The Estimation of Currency Crises Using Artificial Intelligence Methods: The Case of Turkey (2017).*

İlknur Bilgen
She has bachelor's degree from Marmara University Department of Business Administration in 2008. She started working at Hakkari University as an assistant professor in 2017 and she is still working at the same department. She has a master's degree in 2011 and PhD in 2016. Her research areas are marketing, sales management, political marketing, and consumer behavior.

İsmail Ercan Börü
İsmail Ercan Börü was born in Diyarbakır, Turkey. He graduated from Inonu University, Department of Business Administration in 2009. He has a master's degree from University of Birmingham. He graduated from MSc in International Accounting and Finance in 2012. He began PhD about Business Administration in 2016 in Dicle University. He is planning to graduate from PhD in 2020.

List of Tables

List of Figures

Index

www.ingramcontent.com/pod-product-compliance
Ingram Content Group UK Ltd.
Pitfield, Milton Keynes, MK11 3LW, UK
UKHW041829100926
8556IPUK00002B/85

9 783631 798331